"John Henson stands in a long tra
and subversives. Here, he persu
concept of scriptural God has been wrong-headed: that the
Bible is, emphatically, both male and female, and invested in a wide range
of loves that go way beyond the patriarchal and heteronormative. Read
this clever, conversational, learned, and often witty book, and you won't
see the scriptures—or sex and gender—quite the same way ever again."

Glen Retief, Pennsylvania USA,
Professor of Creative non-fiction, Susquehanna University,
author of the Lambda Award-winning The Jack Bank:
A Memoir of a South African Childhood

"John Henson's book THE LOVE LINE is a love letter to a world that
has fractured its relationship with itself. The topic of diversity is usually
thought of from the view of assessing the diversity outside of and around
ourselves, but this book is an invitation to explore the diversity of the
human experience within one's own self by focusing on the kaleidoscope
of gender identities, experiences, and expressions contained in single
a human being. The method John uses to invite the reader into this
adventure is a re-examination of gender, gender roles, and sexuality present
in the themes and narratives of people in the Bible. These familiar stories
that John reframes will amaze and move you. You will resonate with these
new looks at the stories of Eve, Joseph, Ruth, and Jesus, and many more.
It is my hope that reading this book will help heal the internalized limits
to who we can be, how we can move in the world, and whom we can
love. I commend this book especially to the Church, to theologians, and
to all those preparing for ministry. I would love to give this book to every
transgender, non-binary, gender-non-conforming, lesbian, bisexual and
gay young person in the world if I could because it will especially help to
heal the hearts and wholeness of those that patriarchal and homophobic
culture and religion have tried to control and destroy."

Nathan Black,
Master of Divnity.
Christian champion of human rights.
Seattle, Washington, USA.

"Wow! This is a unique, inspiring and liberating book in the broadest and very best sense! John Henson has a wonderful way of seeing things from "outside the box" and in doing so, throughout this amazing and truly prophetic book, he exposes the boxes we are in!. He never shrinks from talking about many issues that christians tend never to broach at all, which is courageous and rare. Moreover, it should be noted from the outset that John has an unusually substantial depth of knowledge of the scriptures - exceptional and outstanding in fact - doubtless gained by having in "Good as New" translated from the original Greek texts himself. So The Love Line is likely to be unacceptable to those people just wanting a good rule book. Underlying the whole work is a lifetime of in-depth pastoral experience, compassion and care for others. Every chapter is so full of meaty substantial material. John points out in depth Jesus' radical inclusion of women; the complete absence of any prudery in Jesus' attitudes, his ability to include gay people as a natural part of society without making us a special interest group. Rather Jesus embraces the whole of humanity in all our diversity, showing us how to live in love together. The Love Line is going to be a wonderful, much-needed, unique resource for the Church; and a huge encouragement for all who have felt marginalised and excluded until now."

Jeremy Marks.
High profile Baptist advocate and befriender of Gay Christians in the UK.
For many years the leader of 'Courage.'

"This is a book sparkling with infectious enthusiasm for the mindblowingly transformative gospel of Jesus. John Henson enables us to leap confidently beyond the narrow and tired debates that characterise so much Christian discussion about gender and sexuality. John reminds us that scripture challenges all attempts to make idols out of human notions of gender norms and so-called family values. John Henson's writing offers a message far more exciting than anything than either religious legalism or secular liberalism can offer."

Symon Hill.
New Testament Scholar
author of 'The Upsidedown Bible'
Oxford UK.

THE
LOVE
LINE

John Henson

Matador
9 Priory Business Park,
Wistow Road, Kibworth Beauchamp,
Leicestershire. LE8 0RX
Tel: 0116 279 2299
Email: books@troubador.co.uk
Web: www.troubador.co.uk/matador
Twitter: @matadorbooks

ISBN 978 1838590 055
British Library Cataloguing in Publication Data.
A catalogue record for this book is available from the British Library.

Printed and bound in Great Britain by 4edge Limited
Typeset in 10.5pt Adobe Garamond Pro by Troubador Publishing Ltd, Leicester, UK

Matador is an imprint of Troubador Publishing Ltd

John Henson wishes to dedicate THE LOVE LINE to all those who have found freedom as Christians to be their true selves and to those who are still seeking to find that freedom.

ABOUT THE AUTHOR

John Henson is a native of Cardiff and a son of the manse. He graduated in history and theology at the universities of Southampton and Oxford (Regent's Park) respectively and was ordained to the Baptist ministry at Carmel Baptist Church, Pontypridd in 1964. He was responsible for a union between his own church and the United Reformed Church in 1969 (now St David's Uniting Church) and has since given assistance to other churches seeking to make similar unions at the local level. He taught history in Cardiff High School from 1970–1973 and then resumed ministry at Glyncoch, Pontypridd in cooperation with the Anglican Communion.

Since 1980 he has been largely freelance, acting as pastoral befriender to people in minority groups while continuing to assist in the conduct of worship in the churches. His interests include music, left-wing politics, penal reform, peace, the quest for truly contemporary and inclusive worship and gender issues. A member of the Lesbian and Gay Christian Movement from its early years, for many years he assisted the movement as the contact person for the South Wales group and as a counsellor. He has lectured on faith and gender in Strasbourg and Oslo at the invitation of the European Union and the World Student Christian Federation. He has also lectured in the UK at universities, ecumenical conferences and retreat centres, at Greenbelt, and at St Michael's Anglican College, Llandaff. He is a member of The Association of Welcoming and Affirming Baptist Churches in the USA. He is keen on Facebook friendship. John is happily married to Valerie, his partner for over fifty years. They have three adult children, Gareth, Iestyn and Rhôda, nine grandchildren – Aidan, Bleddyn, Carys, Gwenllian, Dyfrig, Iona, Isobel, Tomos and Ffion-Medi, and one great grandson – Isaac.

CONTENTS

INTRODUCTION
TO THIS VOLUME

'The Love Line' began as a series of lectures given at the European Union Parliament Building Strasbourg, and the University of Oslo in 1994 and 1995 respectively, the first at the invitation by the European Union and the European Student Christian Federation jointly, and the second on the invitation of the Norwegian Student Federation. On both occasions I was the lead Professor in a conference of leading authorities of that time on the subject of Human Sexuality. My brief was 'Sexuality and the Christian Faith'. On the first occasion it was not intended that I should be the lead Professor. It was to be a week of lectures and I was to lecture on Friday. I received an urgent message on the Monday evening to make immediately for Strasbourg since all the other lecturers has gone down with the 'flu. I caught the train on Tuesday, the Channel Tunnel having only recently been opened, and arrived at Strasbourg late in the evening. For the rest of the week I delivered my set lectures and some more since I had brought extra material with me. I also conducted lots of seminars, tutorials and one-to-one counselling until I was joined by a lecturer from Finland on the Friday. It was hard but exhilarating. There were young people from the highly liberated Sweden and Denmark, as well as from the very conservative Romania and Bulgaria. My experience at Oslo was no less fraught. I was taken ill partway through the conference. I had delivered my main lectures, but missed the chance of mingling with the students. On Saturday I was taken straight out of my sick bed and onto the conference platform to give the final keynote lecture to sum up the whole conference. I did not have a lecture. I had no notes. But I spoke for 45 minutes in a state of trance. My effort was greeted with rapturous applause. I had no idea then nor since of a single word that I said. But it may have been some of the things you will find in the last two chapters of this work. I was subsequently hustled swiftly by car to the Oslo airport, met by my son-in-law Gary with a car at Heathrow, and thence home to Wales. Phew!

CHAPTER ONE

GOD,
THE GENDER BENDER

Gender appears in the very first chapter of the Bible as part of God's creation of the universe. From the very start the concept of gender is ambiguous. Most English translations of Genesis 1:27 produce a translation that goes something like this:

So God created man in his own image, in the image of God he created him; male and female he created them. (NIV)

The suggestion of this translation is that God having created a new species then subdivided it into separate sub-species of male and female. But this is not a correct translation of the Hebrew as most Bibles admit in their margins. What the Hebrew says is:

'God created man in his own image ... male and female he created **him**.*'*

The suggestion is of a single species, a single being containing both male and female characteristics. Indeed, according to the editor who brought together at least two creation stories in Genesis 1 & 2, woman had not at this point been created as a separate entity at all. Whether we accept the original Hebrew or whether we accept our translations' interpretation of what the writer of Genesis was trying to say will make a big difference to our understanding of gender and sexuality. If we follow the translations we will tend to emphasise the distinctiveness and the differences between men and women, whereas if we take the Hebrew writer literally we shall emphasise what men and women share as members of a common species rather than what distinguishes and divides them.

In the text, the possession of masculine and feminine features is closely linked to the idea of being made in God's image. This must mean that features of our humanity we identify as male and female are to be found within the being of God. Indeed, the Hebrew of 1:2 of Genesis talks of God 'brooding over the face of the waters'. God is depicted as a great bird sitting on an egg that is about to hatch. This is a very female picture, except that it should be remembered that male birds of many species also sit on eggs and help to hatch them.

The account of the creation of woman in Genesis 2: 18-23 seems to bear out the Hebrew editor's way of looking at things. When woman has been made out of the man's rib, then man says:-

"This at last is bone of my bones and flesh of my flesh"

Instead of being something separate or additional, woman belongs to the same created species as the man. Their physical composition is the same in most features. In their innocence

2

they are not even aware of the physical differences between the sexes that intrigue and excite us. The comment of the editor that this is why men and women get married also seems to follow the same line. The separation that took place when Adam lost his rib and it became a woman is brought to an end when a man and woman unite again to become 'one flesh'

"Therefore a man leaves his father and mother and clings to his wife, and they become one flesh."

The sexual act is here seen as a way in which the distinction between male and female identities is overcome and the sense of a united single species restored. The overall emphasis is clear. Male and female are not separate, exclusive or rival states, but aspects of a common humanity.

From the point of view of biology this makes sense. Whether we are men or women we have much more in common physically than what distinguishes us. We have two legs, two arms, two eyes, one nose, identical lungs, heart, alimentary canal and so on. It is possible to transplant a heart or kidneys or liver or bone marrow or blood of the right category from a woman to a man. Even in those aspects that we regard as distinct there is what we might call biological cross-dressing. Men have nipples and some men are able to lactate. Women have the clitoris that seems to respond to stimulation in very much the same way as the male penis. In terms of the emotions, both men and women are capable of anger or sorrow, jealousy or hatred, both can love to the point of self-sacrifice, both, as Genesis makes clear, can seduce and be seduced. I am married and have a daughter. As the father I determined her female sex. There is that within me that is capable of producing a female offspring. I also have two sons. My wife had no difficulty in sheltering males in her womb. All three of our children display characteristics that can be traced to one or other of their parents irrespective of sex.

There are many women today who want to reject the Bible because they regard it as a patriarchal book. Others reject it because they consider it to be a homophobic book. It was written by heterosexual men, with the object of re-enforcing and underlining ideas of male superiority and the right to dominate. There is much truth in that view, but it is not the whole truth. Sometimes committees have such strong differences among their members that when finally the report is published, a group within the committee feel the need to produce a 'minority report'. The scriptures were produced by a very large committee. They contain a minority report, and we are only just beginning to pay attention to it. This report follows the suggestion of Genesis that the ideal humanity is not a rampant masculinity (like that which came to bizarre and horrid flowering in Nazi Germany) but rather a humanity based on a harmonious fusion of both male and female. It has some very strong champions in the Hebrew Scriptures, and an even greater champion in Jesus.

When God you spoke your word,
Chaos and darkness heard
And took to flight;
Hear as your children pray
That your Good News today
Will show for each a way;
Give us your light.

Jesus, who came to give
Purpose for all to live,
Healing and sight;

Peace to the sore in mind,
Challenge to dogma blind,
Praise for the good and kind,
    Give us your light.

Spirit on speedy wing,
Giving us songs to sing,
    Fire burning bright;
Loosen our tongues and hearts,
Give to the lost new starts,
And in earth's darkest parts,
    Give us your light.

We know you as the three,
Name you as Trinity,
    Wisdom, love, might;
Help us your peace to share,
Finding you everywhere,
In all who need our care,
    Give us your light.

(John Henson, after John Marriott,
1780-1825 tune: Moscow.)

CHAPTER TWO

MALE CHAMPIONS OF GENDER BENDING

JACOB OR ISRAEL,

is regarded as the prime ancestor of the Jewish race. Jacob was a twin, and in the Biblical account much is made of the contrast between Jacob and his elder twin Esau. Gen.25:27

When the boys grew up, Esau was a skilful hunter, a man of the field, while Jacob was a quiet man, and stayed at home. Isaac, the father, loved Esau because he was fond of game; but Rebekah, the mother, loved Jacob.

Jacob is contrasted with his brother Esau who is all male, a man's man, a hunter, athletic, out-of-doors, his father's pride and joy. Jacob is quiet, reflective, stay-at-home, Mummy's boy. Their temperaments had their correspondence in physical aspects. When Rebekah urged Jacob to deceive his blind father and pose as Esau, Jacob said, "My father will be able to tell the difference by the way I feel to him,-

..my brother Esau is a hairy man, and I am a man of smooth skin. (Gen. 27:11)

This is the Bible, the book some believe to be patriarchic propaganda. The blessing of God is not on the all-male Esau but on the male with a strong admixture of the feminine, Jacob, who takes his mother rather than his father as his role model. He's not only his mother's favourite, he's God's favourite, the one God chooses! As Paul tells his readers in Romans 9: 13:

As it is written "I preferred Jacob to Esau." (GOOD AS NEW)

We should not forget the role of Rebekah in the story. She is the one who is in control of everything, the thinker, the planner, the instrument of God's will, and God's choice. It's the characteristics Jacob gets from his mother, the abilities of foresight and planning, rather than Esau's strength and athleticism, that make Jacob more suitable for God's purposes.

Exiled from home, Jacob falls in love. This is one of the earliest accounts of someone falling in love in history, if not the earliest. Women in the Bedouin society of those days existed for the purpose of providing children and providing the man with an outlet for his male passions. But Jacob fell in love with Rachel. Against the background of that society it was a soft thing to do. He had to wait an inordinately long time for Rachel. (The twice seven years, like most numbers in scripture may be symbolic) He didn't require her, didn't need her for bearing children, in fact she wasn't very good at it. He had another wife and concubines to provide descendents.

Jacob wanted Rachel because he loved her. Rachel is valued for herself. Even her physical beauty must have faded somewhat by the time Jacob got her. But this did not matter to Jacob. It was Rachel Jacob loved, not her body. Few men today would value any woman so highly as to work for seven years in order to make her his marriage partner. This is the value put on someone of the female gender by the patriarch Jacob. When at last Rachel died in childbirth, Jacob transferred his affections to Joseph, the older of Rachel's two boys. Then the pattern of Rebekah and Jacob is repeated, except that this time Jacob is father and mother to Joseph and dotes on him, dresses him up in fancy clothes, and listens to his tales. The others take such a dislike to this girlish little boy that they try to murder him.

When we read these stories we are inclined to view them according to our own cultural standards about how real men should behave. But the Bible tells the stories without any judgements of that kind. Not only is there no condemnation of the feminine elements in the personalities of Jacob and Joseph; they are by implication commended by God, because they are the ones who are successful and transmit the faith of God to future generations. Jacob is not a minor character in the Bible. Jacob is the father of the Israelite people, and in his character both male and female elements combine. This is something he shares with the God he worships. God's Man Jacob is created in the image of God, male and female.

JOSEPH

In Joseph, the son of Jacob and Rachel, we see the most striking example in the scriptures of a trans person. (Better perhaps to say either gender non-conforming person or gender non-binary). Jacob's present to Joseph, which caused such a negative reaction from his brothers, is variously translated (Genesis 37:3) as a 'coat of many colours' (King James Version) a 'long robe with sleeves' (New Revised Standard Version) a' decorated robe' (footnote Good News Bible) 'a richly ornamented robe' (New International Version) or a 'Technicolor dream coat' (Andrew Lloyd Webber). But as Peterson Toscano has pointed out in his highly acclaimed performance, 'Transfigurations—Transgressing Gender in the Bible' the real clue is to be found in 2 Samuel 13: 18, where it is what Princess Tamar, David's daughter, was wearing when serving food to her brother Amnon. We are told that it was what virgin princesses wore, possibly up to and including their bridal night. No doubt Amnon may have excused his crime of rape by calling up Tamar's attire in his defence. What he did was wrong, no matter how provoking her clothing. However this dark incident does throw light back to Joseph. It seems he enjoyed going around wearing and showing off an alluring and seductive princess dress. No wonder his rough uncouth brothers did not regard him as one of them!

Joseph's brothers sold him into slavery in Egypt. As a slave in the nobleman Potiphar's household, Joseph received advances from Potiphar's wife. He was not wearing the princess dress that his father gave him, for the brothers had taken it back to Jacob with goat's blood on it to suggest that a wild animal had killed him. (No DNA tests in those days.) But Joseph may still have been dressing to kill. It has often been suggested that Joseph's ability to resist the mistress of the house's advances may have been less to do with his piety and more to do with not fancying her. Indeed he may not have fancied the opposite sex very much at all. In those days slaves were supposed to do what they were told and keep their mouths shut. Joseph was lucky to get off with just a prison sentence. Joseph's rejection of Lady Potiphar must have wounded her pride. It was also an embarrassing reminder to Potiphar of his own impotence.

Eventually Joseph became second in the land only to Pharaoh himself. As anyone who has seen the portrayals of the Pharaohs may have noticed, they appear to be somewhat gender ambivalent. The male Pharaohs have female shaped buttocks and are heavily made-up. Hatshepsut, a Pharaoh in her own right, wore a false beard. They were highly incestuous, brothers and sisters often marrying each other. We must imagine that Joseph looked very similar to a Pharaoh. He was in his element. So much paint on his face that his brothers did not recognize him.

Despite all of which, he is portrayed in the scriptures as someone who had faith in God, loyal and trusting, and above all loving and forgiving to those who had done him wrong. Peterson believes that in this way he may have expressed his greatest breach of gender roles. Instead of acting as the vengeful male, he instead took on the role of reconciler, thus expanding the options available to men faced with crisis. He becomes the interpreter of God's purposes and the saviour of his own people, and not incidentally, but first and foremost, saviour of the people of Egypt. If, as some scholars think, the story of Joseph was written in the days of the Babylonian captivity or the Persian empire, and added to the book of Genesis, then it shares, with the books of Ruth and Jonah from the same time, an assertion of God's care for the Gentiles. It is at that time that there was a softening in attitude to eunuchs, as so many of the young nobles were castrated when taken into exile. There may also have been a softening towards what today we might refer to as gender non-conforming people.

DAVID

was Israel's greatest king. There was no one to compare with him in his success as a ruler or in his relationship with God. He was also regarded as the role model for future kings, and the Messiah or saviour-figure promised by the prophets would be his descendent and repeat the characteristics of his person and rule. There is no one figure in the scriptures whose personal career is related in such detail and with such honesty as that of David. When we think of his early years we are inclined to think of his killing of Goliath as the most important event. However many scholars think that this story is told of David in order to present him as a man of war, whereas much of the other evidence of David at this period is very different. In 2 Sam. 21:19 we are told that someone called Elhanan killed Goliath and it is likely that David was later given the credit. Although David had the position of King Saul's armour-bearer, it was as court musician that he was most greatly valued. He played the harp and probably sang, and his music usually soothed Saul's nerves. Later on in his career he appeared as an accomplished erotic dancer when he led the celebrations of bringing the Ark to Jerusalem. His success against the Philistines had as much to do with political skill as his skill as a fighter. He often left his military campaigns to his generals, something unheard of for kings of those times. (2 Sam.11:1)

The most important event of David's early years seems to have been his love affair with Jonathan, Saul's son. The records are quite explicit about the nature of this relationship and those who try to make out it was a platonic kind of relationship are not being honest with the texts. It was a relationship of great depth and tenderness and had a physical side to it.

If the writer of the story of David and Jonathan were the slightest bit embarrassed by the relationship he would have toned it down a lot more, and would certainly not have included David's beautiful but revealing poem on the death of Jonathan in battle.

*'I am distressed for you, my brother Jonathan; greatly beloved
were you to me; your love to me was wonderful, passing the love
of women.'* (2 Sam 1:26)

David has no problems in comparing the love between himself
and his friend as that between a man and woman. He takes
woman's love as his ideal, and simply says that Jonathan has
attained it plus plus.

The purpose here is not to debate the question of whether
homosexual relationships are right or wrong in the sight of
God, although this part of scripture quite positively affirms
such a relationship as a good thing. The purpose is to point out
that David, Israel's greatest king and hero, did not regard the
expression of feminine aspects of his personality, or that of his
friend, as anything to be ashamed of, but rather to be proud of
and to immortalize in poetry.

This aspect of David's personality did not disappear with
the death of Jonathan. On the death of his rebellious son
Absalom, David was inconsolable and he couldn't stop crying:

*O my son Absalom, my son, my son Absalom! Would that I had
died instead of you. O Absalom, my son, my son!* (2 Sam: 18:33)

David was a great weeper. He wept with Jonathan. Jacob and
Joseph were also great weepers. On this occasion David disgusted
his troops who wanted to celebrate the victory, and Joab had to
rebuke him and tell him that he was allowing his private grief
to get in the way of his duties as king. The writer, however,
seems to sympathize with David. It is unlikely that he would
have recounted the incident otherwise. If it is feminine to weep,
that's okay, because the great King, especially loved and chosen
by God, was not only masculine but feminine also. God's man
David was made in the image of God, male and female.

One of the titles attributed to Jesus was 'Son of David' which contemporary compatriots of Jesus understood in terms of Jesus being the great king, God's chosen anointed leader figure. But perhaps there were also perceptive folk who were reminded of other aspects of David's character – his personal relationship with God, the special quality of his friendship that inspired the loyalty of others, his forgiving spirit, and his creative artistic temperament.

ISHMAEL

'You are to name him Ishmael, because God has heard of your ill-treatment' (Genesis 16: 11 The Revised English Bible.)

My thoughts here on Ishmael are based on a note my cousin David Henson sent to me on his thinking about the ancestor of the Arab peoples and thence, after a few centuries, the Islamic faith and culture. The two strands with the same distant origin from Abraham are still ill-treating each other, one of the greatest tragedies of human history and a major cause of hostility in our world today. It was common in the culture from which Abraham came for a man to surround himself with several wives and servant concubines to ensure against the failure to repoduce his genes. It was indeed Sarah herself who provided Abraham with Hagar for this purpose. Abraham's first son was therefore Ishmael. He was later joined about 13 years later by Isaac, Sarah's baby. The two boys were circumcised at the same time. Ishmael did not share the feelings of jealousy towards Isaac that Sarah displayed. Indeed he was caught doing a shocking thing, playing with his baby brother, which should have been the task of a nurse maid. Ishmael, the young boy was behaving like a girl, or so it may have seemed. David shared with me the idea that this might amount to the earliest example of a male behaving like a female being thrown out of house and home, and virtually driven to death. For out in the heat of the desert with inadequate provision of water, there would be little hope for mother and son to survive. Whether or not Ishmael displayed feminine traits, he was obviously delicate for his age. He later became an archer, rather than a hand-to-hand fighter, and married a girl from Egypt. And we know how sexually ambivalent the ancient Egyptians were. So perhaps Ishmael had a wife who understood? Albeit, God championed Ishmael and saved his life, and gave the same promise to him that had been given to his father Abraham, that he would be the ancestor of a great nation.

David and I often put our insights into poetry. Here is David's poem which bears witness to the light of Ishmael.

'Father' Abraham.

Father Abraham welcomed strangers
to his shady tent among the oaks,
He met them with bread and cheese,
milk and meat for a feast on his shoulders.
Sojourners transformed into family
by a paternal meal of grace.

Father Abraham dragged his son
to the altar at the mountaintop
He packed no animal, just a flint for fire,
a dagger for blood, a rope for the boy's hands
God transformed into
The Fear
by a paternal act
of terror.

Father Abraham disowned his firstborn, twice,
a teenage boy by then, almost a man,
left to Death in the desert,
because he played with his baby brother
-- bouncing the toddler 'Laughter'
on his knee until giggles spilled out --
instead of doing all the violent things men
must do to the weaker
to prove God must really be
like them.

I wonder if Abraham saw
in Ishmael that day
the father he had always
meant to be.

(David Henson)

CHAPTER THREE

WOMEN CHAMPIONS
OF GENDER BENDING

NAOMI (THE BOOK OF RUTH)

Naomi, the mother-in-law of Ruth, the heroine of the little
book of that name, must be regarded, in her own right, as one
of the pioneers of women's liberation. The book was written to
combat the racism encouraged by Ezra and Nehemiah after the
return of the Jewish exiles from Babylon. Naomi, like the later
exiles, had been forced to live in a 'foreign' country' (Moab).
She was an economic migrant in Moab, driven there by the
famine in her own land of Judah. Her sons married Moabite
women. When death robbed her of both husband and sons,
the only family she possessed in Moab were her two daughters-
in-law, Ruth and Orpah. This was disaster of the highest order

according to the customs of the time. Women had no place in society apart from the men to which they were attached. Males earned and managed income, supported and protected women and children, fought wars, conducted affairs of state and attended to legal matters. Without a man a woman was helpless, adrift. Widows had no option other than find another man as quickly as possible. Otherwise they had to beg. Naomi advised Ruth and Orpah to find new husbands. This advice Ruth refused to contemplate and 'clung' to Naomi, making vows of life-long love and loyalty to her as her chosen partner. It is important to realize that Naomi had no intention of taking her own advice with regard to man hunting. She decided to return to her own country not in order to find a man, but to be at home among her own people and at ease within her own religion. Despite her personal tragedies, she is a figure of great strength. Ruth's love for her and confidence in her are proof. With Naomi as companion Ruth does not need a man, whatever protestations Naomi may make. Naomi and Naomi's God is all the security Ruth requires.

The account seems to suggest that on returning to her native land Naomi adopts a new name. "Don't call me Naomi. Call me Mara." But she is still called Naomi for the rest of the book and we can be sure that is how Ruth continued to address her. Rather than asking to be called by a new name, Naomi is expressing the way she feels and her outlook on life. 'Naomi' means 'pleasant', whereas 'Mara' means 'bitter'. She is saying, "The name you all know me by is not at all suitable, because I don't feel pleasant. The circumstances of life have made me bitter." Naomi has achieved an understanding of herself. Self-knowledge is the first step on the way to strength of character. Even bitterness can be dealt with, if it is faced up to. The people of that day ascribed all the circumstances of life to God, and Naomi did the same. But her bitterness did not only result from her bereavements. It stemmed from awareness of the way the prevailing social structures obliged a woman of spirit to take on the mantle of weakness. So from a strength borne of bitterness she was prepared to play the system to her own and her partner Ruth's advantage. She advised Ruth how to trap a man, not expecting that someone as nice as Boaz would turn up to offer Ruth not just protection and respectability, but true love. She cannot be blamed for allowing her bitterness to be blind to such a possibility, for it was far more likely that a man would desire Ruth simply for her sexual attractiveness and ability to bear children. Neither could Naomi anticipate that the trapped man would spread his love and kindness to include Naomi herself, or that they would all end up as one happy family. Experience was all against such a felicitous outcome. Had things turned out more as she expected, Naomi would have worked to make life bearable for Ruth and herself. She would have ensured a hard bargain with the man and made life difficult for him if he did not prove a good husband to the one on whom fell all her love.

Ruth also was a woman of spirit. She and Naomi were a team. Ruth had youth and beauty; Naomi had experience of the ways of the world. They were a formidable partnership. So we witness, very early on in the history of civilisation, the beginnings of the struggle for women to be taken seriously as human beings. Their witness was not missed, it was not forgotten, it was carried on into the future. It was to take a long time, but eventually such women would carry the day. Ruth, Naomi and Boaz are together at this very moment in the presence of God, smiles on their faces, eyes on the Vatican, watching with fascination the tortuous machinations by which, against all odds, all wickedness and spiritual blindness, women will one day soon achieve equal status with men in the church of Rome, and in all the other churches too.

HANNAH
(1 SAMUEL 1:1—28 & 2: 18-21.)

Hannah was a young woman under a stigma. She had failed to bear children for her husband. If you were in that category you were in trouble in those days. You were labelled 'barren'. It was always the woman's fault. She was under a curse, shunned, derided. Human society has always enjoyed stigmatising people. The Church has often joined in and sometimes been responsible for introducing the stigma. There is no need to cite examples- they are too easy to come by. Hannah's husband Len (Elkanah) had two wives, Hannah and Penny (Peninnah). We are told that Penny would torment and humiliate Hannah 'because the Lord had kept her childless'. She used religion as the whip with which to beat the despised Hannah. One day Len asked Hannah why she was crying. I see him putting his arm around her as he said, "Why are you always so sad? Don't I mean more to you than ten sons?" "Never mind about the children, we've got one another!" In adopting that attitude Len was going against all the prejudice of his day. Wives were for producing children, not for having relationships with! Len's feelings were for his wife in her sorrow and sense of isolation. Len was a modern man. You can almost hear him saying, "Come on, let's do the washing up together; you wash, I'll wipe." Len wore a ribbon for barren wives. He identified himself with them and empathized with their stigma. He treated Hannah not as a barren woman but as a human being.

Hannah took her problem to God, which meant Eli, the priest of Shiloh. Eli represents the opposite type of male from Len. When confronted by a woman in great distress, he concluded she was on the bottle. Throughout the meeting between Hannah and Eli, Hannah comes across as emotionally and spiritually more mature than Eli. She had to explain her 'women's problems' to

Eli painstakingly, as if to a child. He got there in the end and gave her his 'blessing'. Hannah also displayed a technique of prayer in advance of her time. She puzzled Eli by praying silently. Prayer in ancient times was always aloud, which was why the Pharisees could use it is a means of showing off and why Jesus advised people to find a private place to pray. There was no medical treatment in those days whereby the barren could be enabled to give birth. No doubt there were plenty of old folk remedies. A priest's blessing was held to be effective. Eli's blessing proved to be so. In an age when there was no IVF treatment, or sperm available in a test tube from an anonymous donor or someone in the family, we must not be shocked if the truth was that the priest provided a service over and above a prayer. The priest was a holy man, and to unite with him in such circumstances and for this limited purpose would have been thought a holy act, and not at all unethical. It is common today, after giving birth as a result of artificial insemination, for a woman then to go on to produce children in the normal way. Hannah may have benefited from a more natural version of this technique. Our sense of outrage arises in part from our lack of appreciation of the therapeutic aspect of sex, thanks to the repressive teaching of the Church on the subject. Christians continue to be ill at ease with regards to fertility treatment.

Hannah composed the Magnificat. Today it is attributed to Mary, the mother of Jesus, who simply adapted it. It was not Mary's song even in the adapted version, since Mary sang it for joy when she learned of the pregnancy of her cousin Elizabeth who had experienced the same stigma as Hannah. Indeed the song was likely used from the time of Hannah on in services of thanksgiving when the barren conceived. In both Hannah and Mary's version the song is surprisingly not so much about having babies as about revolution. It's about a changed world where all stigmas are done away with. Hannah sings,

'He lifts the poor from the dust and raises the needy from their misery. He makes them companions of princes and puts them in the places of honour.''

People who have been stigmatised are hypersensitive to the burden of the stigma carried by others.

In order to conceive Hannah did a deal with God. That was unwise, but Hannah was desperate.

"If you give me a son, I promise that I will dedicate him to you for his whole life." (v 11)

That meant that as soon as the child was weaned he would be taken to the house of the Lord, where he would stay to his dying day. (v22) It was a terrible bargain. Samuel was torn from his mother's love before he had chance to get to know her and was put in the charge of Eli at the shrine at Shiloh. Eli may have been the biological father, but he was old, half blind, notoriously a bad parent whose two sons were not nice to know. The main operation in the shrine where this young child would be expected to assist was the grisly business of animal sacrifice. The Sunday School picture of Samuel is of the pure young child, instructed by Eli, listening for God's word and so on. In fact he turned out to be a nasty piece of work. There is more than one kind of abuse and today, without doubt, Samuel would be identified by a psychiatrist as a victim of abuse. Did Hannah ever regret her foolish promise to God? Did she ever shed a tear? You bet she did – more tears than she shed when she had no child at all. We have such a sad little picture of Hannah visiting Shiloh once a year to give him the new coat she had made.

The story of Hannah is such a mixture. We have the story of a stigmatized woman, in part consoled by a sensitive husband in touch with his feminine side. She is a woman with spirit, articulate, artistic and creative. She towers above Eli in spirituality. Together with her loving husband, Hannah looks forward to a new humanity free from stigmas, free from prejudice, free to appreciate people for what they are and what they can contribute. The story also serves as a warning, that wherever that ideal is not fully attained, there will always been victims. There will always be those, like Samuel, whose personalities are forever wounded. There will always be those like Hannah, with aching hearts.

1) The morn was breaking in,
the holy tent still dark;
The oil lamp burning dim
Before the sacred box,
When suddenly a voice divine
Spoke through the silence of the shrine.

2) The priest, unkempt, uncouth,
In charge of Shiloh, slept;
Nearby an anxious youth
A wakeful watch still kept;
And what from Eli's sense was sealed,
God unto Hannah's son revealed.

3) We envy Samuel's ear,
An open ear, dear God,
Alive and quick to hear
Your whispers, word by word.
Like him we would obey your call,
And stay close to you, most of all.

4) We envy Samuel's heart,
A patient heart that waits,
Ready your work to start,
Never to help found late;
A heart that always, night or day,
Will not from caring turn away.

5) But, no, much more we crave,
For Samuel comes not near
One who has love to save
From anger, guilt and fear.
The One who was all hate above
And came to teach us how to love.

(After 'Hushed was the evening hymn' J.D.Burns,
based on 1 Samuel chapter 3.)

ESTHER is an example of a woman in the Bible who dared to invade a man's world. The background is the Persian court of King Ahasuerus. The book of Esther has to do with racism. Before Esther makes her bold stand in defence of her people and in defence of her own personal value, the way is prepared for her by her spiritual sister Vashti, first queen of Ahasuerus. Vashti was commanded by the drunk king to appear before his courtiers to demonstrate her beauty. We can imagine what the king is going to require of her. She refuses. She will not be treated as a sex object by a crowd of drunken, lecherous men. This brave stand unnerves the men. One of them says that if this is allowed to go unpunished all the women in the land will start refusing to obey their husbands. (Esther 1:16 ff) So Vashti is dismissed and a proclamation made that all women are to honour their husbands from now on. Exceedingly insecure behaviour!

Esther, a Jewess, now replaces Vashti as queen. Mordecai, her stepfather uncovers a plot to exterminate the Jews. He asks her to intercede with the king for the Jewish people. The problem is that Esther cannot approach the king unless he calls for her. To do so would be to step out of line, just as Vashti had done. But Esther goes ahead. It is an act of solidarity not only with her own people, but also with Vashti and all other women who are treated as slaves by men. After a tense moment the king stretches forth his sceptre, allowing Esther to approach. After this Esther takes her full place as queen – the king offers her half the kingdom. They work together to govern the state and to defeat the racists.

Esther is perhaps a minor figure against the whole background of scripture. But she is credited with responsibility for the creation of the festival of Purim. Most of the other Jewish festivals are regarded as having been instituted by Moses. She is in very high company indeed. As well as being a saviour of her own people, Esther was a pioneer of the liberation of her sex, a step along the road whereby the humanity of God's creation could become complete. Both male and female sit side by side on the throne and have equal influence in the government of society. Esther and Ahasuerus who, under the guidance of Esther, is himself liberated, are part of humanity made in the image of God, male and female.

The position of women with regard to the Genesis declaration about gender is different from that of men. With men it is a matter of being in touch with the feminine side of their nature and allowing it to develop. For women it is matter of asserting that they are full members of the human race and not just the property of men. Women have to claim as a natural right the privileges, responsibilities, freedoms and choices that men have always taken for granted. Sometimes this has to be done with an energy traditionally understood as masculine, and in this way perhaps women discover their masculine instincts at the same time as they seek a true respect for their femininity. But for both men and women it means becoming complete people and not being victims of the strict division between male and female behaviour and consciousness that many societies expect.

Chapter four

Jesus,
the Gender Bender

Jesus is described by Paul and by the writer to the Hebrews (possibly Priscilla) as 'The Image of God' (2 Cor.4:4; Col. 1:15 Heb.1:3) Thus Jesus represents what God intended when God brought humankind into being. Jesus's own title for himself was 'Son of Man' – 'Child of Humanity', which was an ambiguous title possibly meaning Messiah, but more likely expressing the identification of Jesus with humanity as a whole. (In Good As New "The Complete Person.")

We are badly served by the Christmas card image of the holy family. Mary is always seated, holding the baby, while Joseph stands behind watching benevolently. Why not Joseph holding the baby with Mary watching? It is not always the Bible that is responsible for our patriarchal stereotypes. We know even less of Joseph than we know of Mary, but in the story where he appears in the family visit to Jerusalem when Jesus was twelve, he and Mary act together as equals. Mary says, "Look, your father and I have been searching for you in great anxiety." As parents they are partners, a team!

In his life and ministry Jesus demonstrated a revolutionary approach to women and an integration of the feminine with the masculine in his own character and behaviour. The regular daily prayer of the Jewish male was "I thank you God I am not a Gentile, a Slave or a Woman." Women were inferior, they were discounted, marginalized. Jesus made all classes of the oppressed his priority targets, including women. Luke makes it quite clear in Chapter 8 that Jesus had female as well as male disciples. Luke only knows some of the names, but tells us there were others. Big Mary (Maggie), Joan, Susan and others are described as being 'with him', the technical term for a disciple. (Mark 3:14) Mary Dategrove is commended to her sister Martha for sitting at the feet of Jesus, the disciple's place, and Martha is called to join her.

To the leader of the synagogue who protests when Jesus heals a disabled woman on the Sabbath Day, Jesus says, "You would do more for your ox or your donkey than you are prepared to do for this woman. She is a daughter of Abraham." She thus has the potential for a direct relationship with God, to speak in God's name, and communicate God's blessing, like her illustrious ancestor. (Lk. 13:15ff)

It's his natural human sympathy with the women Jesus encountered that sets Jesus apart as someone quite remarkable and radical. Jesus refuses to condemn the female sex offender who is brought before him for judgement. The implication of the story is that Jesus disapproves of the system in which it is the woman who is taken hold of and punished for adultery. Where was the man involved? To the men who gathered round for judgement Jesus says, "Let **him** who is without sin cast the first stone!" They slink away one by one. (Jn. 8: 1-11) Just as the men must not be excused from their parenting role in the family, so men must not escape blame when they put the family at risk. All the men in the story are involved. The invisible adulterous man, obviously, and also the male accusers. For whereas if the peccadillo were kept secret the family might yet survive and move on, if it is made public, no chance!

The way Jesus mixed easily and freely with women was a source of astonishment to his followers. They were surprised to find him talking to the woman of Samaria at the well (Jn.4). Both were unaccompanied – scandalous behaviour by the standards of the day. Prostitutes were among the bad company Jesus kept and brought the scorn of his critics the Pharisees (e.g. Mk. 15:1). According to Jesus, prostitutes would get into the Kingdom before the God Squad. (Mat.21:31)

Two stories graphically illustrate the special sympathy Jesus had with the feminine sex. On one occasion a woman touched the cloak of Jesus in order to get healing. (Mk. 5:25ff) The woman suffered from haemorrhages. Women were regarded as being ritualistically unclean when they had their monthly periods. (This argument is still used for barring women from the priesthood!) This woman had a perpetual period, so she was perpetually unclean. She should not have been in public and certainly not touching a man. Jesus insisted on identifying her for the purpose of freeing her from her guilt and isolation. She is not only healed; she is also told to "go in peace". At the point when the woman touched Jesus, the gospel-writer tells us that Jesus felt power going out from him. (v.30) Male commentators have always assumed this means that when Jesus healed he was somehow physically weakened as power passed from him to the patient, though nowhere else is this suggested in the healing ministry of Jesus. It seems more likely that Jesus, with his unique hypersensitivity, experienced the sense of the constant draining of life that the woman was feeling. Jesus was entering into the woman's experience of the monthly period with its attendant loss of energy. By implication he condemns the ritual isolation of women on that account. This is a sensitive and embarrassing area for some women. Jesus was completely at ease and competent in dealing with it. The woman could not have done better had she gone to a woman doctor!

The other story is that of the so-called 'sinful' woman who interrupted the meal when Jesus was being entertained by Simon the Pharisee. (Lk. 7:36) By 'sinner' was almost certainly meant 'prostitute'. She was probably already well known to Jesus, though the Pharisee did not expect them to be acquainted. This woman put on a disgraceful act of familiarity with Jesus. Without any inhibitions she expressed her love for him. She did this in the way she was most familiar with, using all the techniques of her trade. She unbuttoned her hair to use it as a towel; she gave Jesus a head massage and a foot massage with aromatic oils; she kissed him not once but non-stop, over and over again. I suspect very few Christians today would be able to witness this sight without feeling embarrassed or even sick.

How do we imagine Jesus behaved in this situation? Did he freeze? Was his role in the encounter completely passive? That would go against the whole sense of the account. Surely Jesus also gently returned her affection and touching. Jesus accepted and affirmed this woman as she was. He accepted with joy her love, her physicality, and her particular gifts so despised or disapproved of by others.

Jesus pointedly contrasted the behaviour of the woman towards him with the behaviour of his host. "You didn't wash my feet; you didn't give me a kiss- not even one; you didn't give me a massage!" (v46) What is Jesus suggesting? Is he suggesting that it would be right and proper for Simon, a man, to behave towards him in this physically intimate way? Jesus is the 'Complete Person'. He not only affirms the value and quality of a woman's techniques of love, but also recommends them to a man as appropriate for him to copy and use in relationship with another man.

Jesus showed the same kind of freedom in his dealings with other men as he did in his dealings with women. John's Gospel contains frequent references to a man referred to as 'the disciple Jesus loved'. The Church made up its mind too quickly with regard to many of the mysteries of scripture with the result that we have often got stuck with one narrow interpretation. Because John, son of Zebedee, was thought to be the author of the gospel, and because he is not mentioned by name in its pages, it was early assumed that 'disciple Jesus loved' is a pseudonym for John. It is a convenient way of avoiding the obvious that for many Christians conflicts with their taboos. The straightforward explanation is that there was a man who Jesus loved more strongly and more intensely than the rest of his friends and that this was an open secret to those who knew him well. Because of our problems about two people of the same sex loving one another, we try to imagine a not very convincing relationship devoid of any physical, sexual or intensely emotional aspects. (Those who can shake their minds free of the misinformation they have inherited will eventually notice that the 'Beloved Disciple' is clearly introduced in chapter 11 and identified as the disciple Jesus loved twice, in order to make sure the reader gets it.)

The gospels have a different view of Jesus from Paul's. They are based on the memories of people who actually met Jesus. Paul is hardly interested in Jesus the human being at all. Jesus is important for the role he plays as saviour, divine sacrifice, mediator and so on. The gospels portray the love of Jesus for men and women on every page, and the love Jesus shows is a love of physical and emotional involvement.

When the rich young man came to Jesus to ask the secret of entry into the kingdom, Mark comments, "Jesus looked at him and loved him." (MK.10:21) The comment seems almost irrelevant to the story. There must have been some special way Jesus looked at the young man that left its impression on those who were watching, and it must have been a strong impression. In my country especially, men are wary of looking at one another and get uptight when looked at intently by one of their number. They hate the thought that they may be attracted by or attractive to another man. Jesus did not share this inhibition. (It must be at least 50% likely that this young man was the Beloved Disciple. It's the only instance in the gospels where Jesus is specifically described as loving a particular man apart from Lazarus (Larry). Significantly Matthew and Luke, who copy much of Mark's gospel, including this story, leave out Mark's mention that Jesus' love of the young man was in the first instance inspired by a physical attraction. They are obviously uneasy about it.

Jesus sympathized with the centurion who expressed a strong love for his male servant. (Matt. 8:5ff) According to the traditions of the Roman army the relationship may well have had a physical side to it, which could account for the guilt the centurion expresses when he says he is not worthy to have Jesus under his roof. Jesus showed no sign of disapproval but rather commended the soldier for his faith. (We know the practice of sexual male bonding was common in the Roman army because the Emperor Augustus tried to put a stop to it. There was no chance of him being successful, especially not since he was succeeded by Tiberius whose stance on the matter of homosexuality was quite different from that of the puritanical Augustus, to put it mildly. Tiberius was Emperor at the time of Jesus.)

At the grave of his friend Larry Jesus wept. It was customary to weep in the face of death. But something about the weeping of Jesus brought comment from the bystanders, "See how he loved him!" Jesus 'snorted like an angry bull' and 'sounded like a dog howling in distress'. (GOOD AS NEW) Others thought Jesus was putting on an act. Either way, it must have been an exceptional sight. Jesus, like David, was a great weeper. Like David's tears for Absalom, the tears of Jesus were extravagant in the opinion of his contemporaries. Jesus also wept over the city of Jerusalem. (Lk.19:41).

"O Jerusalem, Jerusalem, you who kill the prophets and stone those sent to you, how often have I longed to gather your children together as a hen gathers her chicks under her wings, but you were not willing." (Lk.13:34)

This is the cry of the rejected lover whose embraces are spurned. Jesus, like the Spirit of God in Gen.1, pictures himself as the mother hen. Hebrews tells us "During the days of Jesus's life on earth, he offered up prayers and petitions with loud cries and tears." The freedom with which Jesus wept was something eyewitnesses remembered.

But you too, good Jesus, are you not also a mother?
Are you not a mother who like a hen gathers her chicks
beneath her wings? ...
And you, my soul, dead in yourself,
run under the wings of Jesus your mother
and lament your griefs under his feathers.
Ask that your wounds may be healed
and that, comforted, you may live again.
Christ, my mother, you gather your chickens under your wings...

(Anselm of Canterbury, a monk who lived from 1033-1109 C.E. quoted in *She Who Is,* by Elizabeth A. Johnson)

In the account given in John's gospel of the final meal between Jesus and his followers, Jesus is portrayed as taking a towel and a basin and washing the disciples' feet. (John 13) Jesus then invites the disciples to take him as their role model.

"...if I, your Leader and Teacher, have washed your feet, you ought also to wash one another's feet."

We should not assume that because the women disciples are not specifically mentioned they were not present. The disciples were to accept Jesus as the role model. Where did Jesus get his role model? It has usually been assumed that he got his model from the slave who would normally perform the foot washing as guests arrived for a meal. Thus 'foot washing' is sometimes referred to as the sacrament of service. But this foot washing takes place in the middle of a meal. It is an interruption. The role model is the woman who interrupted the meal to express her love for Jesus, either as in Luke's account where she is identified as a prostitute or in John's account where she is Mary of Bethany, a woman disciple who comes in for condemnation by those present because of her waste of precious oils. So this is not the sacrament of service but the sacrament of physical contact. The hymn 'a touching place' is more in keeping as an accompaniment than 'kneels at the feet of his friends'. Rocky protests, "You will never wash my feet." Since the prostitute and Mary of Bethany are the role models, Rocky is not saying, "You shouldn't be acting the slave like this, Jesus," but something like, "Get off, you great poof. I'm a real man- I don't appreciate that kind of thing!"

The reply of Jesus takes us full circle to Genesis 1. "Unless I wash you, Rocky, you cannot become part of me." The washing brings one person into union with another, as also the sacrament of eating and drinking for which the foot washing is sometimes seen as the alternative in John's Gospel. It belongs to the same agenda as the uniting of the first human pair. It involves the destruction of stereotypes that divide the sexes and make true union impossible, whether between a man and a woman or between a man and another man. Rocky is a character of extremes – the nickname was probably meant with a tinge of humour. From protesting, Rocky goes to the opposite extreme, -,

"In that case, Jesus, you had better wash me all over." "That won't be necessary", says Jesus, "you visited the public baths on the way here. I only need to wash your feet!"

The account of the foot washing is preceded by a piece of theology from the gospel-writer:

'Jesus, knowing...that he had come from God and was going to God.'(v.3)

Jesus brings from God the image of God, God's portrait, which comprises a harmony of male and female. He returns to God as "The Complete Person" who contains within his knowledge and experience both of what it means to be a man and what it means to be a woman. Jesus also performed to perfection the male role, as traditionally understood. Jesus was the head of the household, responsible for the family, widened in his case to the family of humankind. He cared for the weak and enfeebled, organized a movement and a mission, and took up the cross, a very male mode of execution. We must say 'male role as traditionally understood', because there is no reason why all these aspects of humanity should not be fully performed by women. Male and female roles are largely a matter of tradition and social conditioning.

What do these new insights and discoveries about Jesus mean for us and today's church and society? You may think I have been hinting that Jesus was 'gay'. If so, you have missed the point. He was neither 'gay' nor a 'radical feminist' as we understand those terms nowadays. The gay experience and the feminist experience, which came so much to the fore in of the twentieth century, are a striving after what Jesus was aiming at. Both are inadequate and incomplete answers to the problem of a humanity over-divided and stressed by the concepts of male and female. The division of a single humanity into 'male and female' has been further divided into 'gay and straight male' and 'gay and straight female' and subdivided again into 'gays who play the female role' and 'those who play the male role' and so on and so on. Gay liberation has been instrumental in giving all males extra options. Men, straight as well as gay, can now wear colourful clothes , including pink, and jewellery. They can use cosmetics and deodorants and style their hair, if they choose. They can arrange flowers or refuse to be interested in sport without adverse comment except from the extremely ignorant. Women are on the way to competing in all the professions on equal terms with men as a result of the feminist movement. Great gains! When society and church are fully at ease with the truth that the love that comes from God can be expressed and channelled between partners of the same sex, we will have made a massive step towards heaven on earth!

But the aims of Jesus will not be attained whilst the divisions male, female, gay, straight cause people to huddle together in separate groups with rival and competing areas and life-styles. The aim of Jesus is for a society that holds within it the maximum variety of responsible and loving human expression, where each expression is regarded and valued by all as part of their common humanity. On the individual level, the aim of Jesus is for everyone to own and value those elements within themselves that they see expressed in others who may yet be very different from them. This means we may all have loving same-sex relationships and may all have loving relationships with the opposite sex, though what that entails will differ widely from relationship to relationship. But we shall all regard all types of relationship as an expression of the humanity we hold in common with others. There will be no need for ghettos created for the comfort and ease of specific types. We shall all be at ease and comfortable with one another. Though we do not seek a particular relationship, we shall be at one with those who do, and enter into their joy when they find it. Judgemental jealousy and envy will cease. God made us female and male. If we deny their full expression either within ourselves or within the society of which we are part, we are inadequate half-people. The purpose of God in Jesus is that male and female become one humanity: that the two become one flesh.

Jesus Comes, But Do You See Him?

Jesus comes, but do you see him?
Incognito now his way.
Very plainly told his followers
He would never go away.
"I will be with you" (x3)
God in Christ has come to stay.

Every eye shall now behold him
In the faces of the poor;
We may catch him in the stranger
Who comes knocking at our door.
Will we recognize him? (x3)
Gently knocks, has knocked before.

Do you see him in the children
You abuse with hate and fear?
There is more than just one way
To mistreat a life so dear.
Jesus offers Good News (x3)
Not your sin-soaked doctrines drear

.

And where two or three are gathered,
Not to boast their claim on grace,
But to plan their help for others,
Then he will be in that place.
Just as he promised (x3)
Jesus shines in each kind face.

So if there ever comes a special day
When he's seen by all the world;
Folk of every kind processing;
Multi-coloured flags unfurled-
Some will be puzzled (x3)
Those who spot him will be thrilled.

(Alternative to Charles Wesley's 'Lo he comes.'
John Henson Advent 2014)

CHAPTER FIVE

WHO WAS THEN A GENTLE MAN?

*'When Adam delved and Eve span,
who was then the gentleman?'*

(John Ball 1381)

We are getting there at last, but the pace is painfully slow. Despite liberation movements, despite all sorts of changes in social behaviour and in the laws towards the end of the century before this one, equality or 'even balance' between the sexes is still some way off. Fears that one day the female sex might get the upper hand are still the stuff of science fiction. The institutional Church, as throughout most of history, tends to reflect not the society that has recently passed away, but the one before that. In no senses is this a joke. There is usually a small but vocal minority of eccentrics pestering the Church to get a move on, regarded by the rest as irresponsible. These tend to be firmly marginalized and denied any power or platform within the system.

The pace at which the Church moves is slowed down not only by its instinctive erring on the side of safety, but also by the weight of its own body of traditions, chief among them 'Holy Scripture'. The only scriptures taken much notice of were written two thousand years ago, despite the fact that Christians, many of them great minds, have been writing continually since. In actual fact it is not the scriptures themselves, old or new, that hold us back, but their interpretation, which constantly changes, but always cautiously, slowly and sometimes backwards. Movements like the Reformation or the discovery of the methods of 'higher criticism' in the nineteenth century, caused much excitement and very unchristian strife at the time, but in retrospect were not as revolutionary as all that. More dead weight was retained than jettisoned. Those who were sure they had in the Bible a staunch ally in their assumptions of male dominance came easily through these times without the slightest cause for alarm. Some feminists, understandably fed up by now, have concluded that the Bible as it stands can never be anything but a hindrance to those who seek a Christian community in which women take their rightful place as true leaders and not just loyal supporters. Until very recently it was assumed the Bible was written exclusively by males. It has certainly always been translated that way, every word, every nuance, given a masculine slant. But the number of books we can guess might have been written by a woman is growing all the time. The assured movements in society towards genuine equality, and the appreciation of the riches brought to human self-knowledge by the inclusion of feminine and gay ways of looking at things, are coming to the Church's rescue, though the Church cannot see it like that. The new perspectives light up every aspect of life and culture including religion, whether religion likes it or not. We are just beginning to see, those of us who are trying, things in scripture we have been incapable of seeing before, highly encouraging to feminist and gay aspirations- no thanks to our clerical hierarchies, or even much to our theological colleges, but to she who is the Holy Spirit speaking in our world.

ADAM AND EVE

The story of Adam and Eve, not forgetting the snake, has been used by the Church throughout the ages for the subjugation and embarrassment of women. It was Eve who 'tempted' Adam, resulting in his fall. She is therefore cursed and henceforth mistrusted as a seducer, a dangerous influence whose advice is to be resisted. One response to the story is to say, "This story dates from very primitive times; it has nothing to say to us in the twenty first century. It is anti-women and deserves to be set on one side." That would be a mistake. For a fresh look at the ancient allegory shows that the popular résumé of the plot is a complete travesty, and that far from showing woman in an unfavourable light vis-à-vis the man, it does the opposite.

In the first chapter of Genesis, humankind is the climax of creation. The sequence marks an upward progression from energy to matter, matter to simple life forms, vegetable life followed by animal life, from sea creatures to reptiles and upward to mammals and finally ourselves. A brilliant anticipation of Darwin! The editor of the book of Genesis intends us to conclude that what comes later is a higher form of creation from the earlier. In Genesis chapter 2, 'man' is created first, 'woman' second. Although scholars believe this story has a separate origin from the story of chapter one, the editor intends us to read the stories as a sequence. Thus it is woman, not man, who turns out to be the summit of creation! "When God created man she was just practising." (Rita May Brown)

According to the story in Genesis, the creation of woman is a response by God to man's need. God says, "It is not good for the man to live alone." We have a statement of man's inadequacy, which it seems cannot be entirely answered by animals or vegetables. Taking the dog for a walk or talking to the potted plants is not the answer to a man's loneliness. Only God's special and super creation will do the trick.

Again, at this point, the traditional interpretation casts the woman in the inferior role. The woman is described as man's 'helper' (RSV & NIV). This conjures up the picture of someone to do the cleaning and ironing, to get his meal ready, and to put out his slippers when he comes home from work. However the Hebrew word (ezer) means something like 'to save from extremity' or 'deliver from death' and outside this passage is only used of God. In Psalm 33 where the picture is that of warfare, 'God is our <u>succour</u> and shield'. Woman is not some kind of menial or pliant assistant. She is essential to man's survival and well being. Far from being dependant on man (an idea often deduced from 'the rib'), man is dependent on woman in much the same way as he is dependent on God. She is his 'saviour'. When the woman has been created and is alive and aware, while man still lies helpless, we read that God 'caused the woman to come towards the man.' This is not a description of servitude, but describes woman taking the initiative. Eve is pro-active; Adam is re-active. The verb used is often found in a sexual situation and usually describes the advances of the male to the female in courtship and lovemaking. At the beginning, in what the editor regards as the ideal state of affairs, woman proposes. It is the norm, not a comical reversal as in our Leap Year custom.

This is followed by the startling comment by the editor, to be quoted for its importance by Jesus, 'Therefore the man will abandon his father and mother and cleave to his woman.' We have reversed this pattern in our western marriage services. The bride comes down the aisle on the arm of her father (or stand-in male equivalent), as if she cannot manage it on her own. Scandalously and disgracefully, in many of our churches, including some which should know better, she continues to be handed over from one family to another as if she were a piece of property, which of course she has allowed herself to be. Whereas, according to Genesis and Jesus, it was God's idea that it should be the man who changes loyalties He should become attached to his wife rather than his wife to him.

And so we come to the snake, which Christians have been inclined to interpret as inordinate animal instincts, sex in other words. Freud played along with this, understanding the snake in the Garden of Eden, like the snakes in our dreams, as the penis or the fear thereof. For the author/authors of Genesis, the snake was more likely the symbol of the rival Canaanite religions, for they involved the worship of snake images. However the author you are at present having the patience to read has suggested in 'Other Temptations of Jesus' a different role for the snake. I quote myself:

*'what part does the snake play in the story? Tempter?…a dire warning to make you wary of life, forever on your guard, forever inhibited and uptight?…**the snake is a welcome third voice** in a debate which enables the first pair to stop mooching about in a garden and come to their first adult decision.'* (Chapter 10, page 113)

Like Satan in the book of Job, but not to be confusedly identified with Satan, the snake acts as a think tank, widening the range of alternatives and opportunities, and enabling sentient humans to move towards the destiny God has in mind for them anyway. Their future is to be free spirits, like to God's self. The snake helps them cultivate a feeling for adventure and risk taking, despite the instinct they also possess that they may get into trouble. The person who never made a mistake, never made anything. Even God, at one point, came to the conclusion that making humans had been a mistake, according to Genesis. (Chapter 6: 6-7)

But we must examine more closely the conversations between the humans and the serpent thought provoker. The snake makes a suggestion to the woman; the woman passes on the suggestion to the man, and the die is cast. The idea that the woman, by means of sexual allure, causes man's downfall in this way is ludicrous, and quite without foundation in the text. The couple are not even aware of their sexual distinctions until after they have eaten the fruit. If we concentrate on the content of the conversation we must come to an entirely different view of the woman. The woman is portrayed as the thinker and the one with the religious sensibilities. She has taken note of God's words and quotes them to the snake in much the same way as Jesus quotes God's words to the devil in the desert. The man appears to have forgotten what God said and has his mind on his next meal. Eve was far from being a pushover. The snake was 'subtle'. He had to be subtle, otherwise he would have stood no chance. In contrast, when the woman brings the fruit to her husband, he eats without a word of protest. It is the man, not the woman, who is closest to the animal and a slave to his appetites. We are put in mind of Adam's descendant Esau who sold his inheritance for a bowl of soup. His brother Jacob, however, was a spiritual descendant of Eve as well as of Adam.

Jacob took after his mother and knew how to argue, how to plan, and how to make decisions, for good or ill. Even if this story is interpreted along traditional lines, the balance of guilt for doing wrong falls more decisively on the man's side. Eve eats because she has reflected and been convinced by an argument; Adam eats because he is thoughtless. The way Adam tries to put all the blame on his wife, unloading the responsibility, shows he is no gentleman. If he had not left his religious duties to his wife (a very contemporary syndrome), together they may have been a match for the serpent, or at least been prepared to own up and face the consequences afterwards.

Finally, traditional interpretations have dwelt on the woman's curse, almost ignoring the man's curse. The 'curse', an unfortunate set of handicaps, is caused by the behaviour of Adam and Eve. The curse is not God's intention and purpose for humankind, and God's plans stay in place whatever may occur. So the handicaps are not to be understood as chains in which men and women are inevitably and permanently bound, but as a challenge to them to break free and achieve God's original idea for them. They have lost Eden. They have the opportunity, if they co-operate with God, to turn earth into Eden again. The second part of the woman's curse, "Your desire shall be for your husband and he shall rule over you" is, as part of the curse, not a revelation of divine law, but a reversal of God's scheme. In God's scheme the woman is man's saviour, not his helpless victim. Woman is thereby called through the curse to struggle towards her original destiny. In the same way, sexual prudery is not a good thing. Humankind is called to regain the ideal of innocence, to overcome the curse of abusive and exploitative sex, and to discover the joy of sex as God's gift.

CHAPTER SIX

CAIN AND ABEL

(Genesis chapter 4. Qur'an chapter 5: 27-)

The story of Cain and Abel in chapter 4 of Genesis appears to be a continuation of the story of Adam and Eve. However it is probably a story from another tradition with no connection with Adam and Eve whatsoever. The editor who is weaving his own story, connects it to Adam and Eve by making Cain and Abel the first children of Adam and Eve. The editor's intention is to show how Adam and Eve's estrangement from God leads inevitably to the first act of inhumanity of one human being to another. This creates lots of problems for literalists, not least the question of where Cain got his wife. The story, however, is more likely to reflect the later rivalry in the Promised Land between the Hebrew peoples who at first dealt primarily with livestock, and those who were in the land before them who were primarily crop growers. Cain the agriculturalist was the elder having arrived first and Abel the shepherd was the younger having arrived later. One possible meaning of the name Abel may be 'herdsman' . It is like the Arabic *'ibil'* which now means 'keeper of camels'. Cain may mean 'metal smith'. Agriculture required machinery made of metal, plough shares and pruning hooks. So did warfare. God accepted Abel's sacrifice of an animal, and not Cain's offering from his grain crop. It was the Hebrews and not the Palestinians who were God's true people. Another possibility is that it's a story intended to explain the origins of the Kenite tribe, which became part of Israel and was merged into the tribe of Judah. (e.g. 1 Sam.27:10) Scholars also believe that the Kenites were the same as the Midianites. Jethro, Moses' father-in-law was the priest of Midian, and it may be that from the Midianites/Kenites that Moses got his monotheistic religion There were never exactly twelve tribes. The number twelve was symbolic and preserved artificially by dividing tribes or putting tribes together. Thus the story of Cain might have been not so much a moral tale as a story to explain how people of differing cultures happened to be side by side, or in conflict. (Other merged tribes included Kenizzites, Jerahmeelites, Calebites, Othnielites and Gibeonites) The editor provides the moral flavour to the story.

There are two parts to the story. The first story recounts the murder of Abel. The second tells what happens to Cain afterwards. Both stories tell of God's care for both brothers, for all humanity.

The first part of the story has to do with violence. Both the brothers are religious. Being religious does not of itself get you anywhere. In fact, being religious got neither of these brothers anywhere at all. We are not told exactly why God was impressed by Abel's offering and not by Cain's. We imagine that the editor has gone beyond the primitive idea that God liked nothing better than a roast lunch, and preferred it to breakfast cereal. The first hearers of the story, sitting around a camp fire would imagine a picture in their mind of two altars, one with some meat cooking, with white pillar of smoke going up in a straight line to heaven, and God having a pleasing sniff; the other with a burning bundle of hay with black smoke blowing in all directions, and God having a fit of coughing. The editor however, like the prophet Samuel in the case of the chosen David and his unchosen brothers, believes that 'God looks on the heart'. That's a good New Testament idea. The New Testament begins in the Hebrew scriptures, not with the Gospels. Samuel's words are reflected in the old harvest hymn:

> 'No gifts have we to offer
> For all your love imparts
> But that which thou desirest,
> Our humble, thankful hearts.'

Maybe Abel had a humble, thankful heart. Maybe he looked at the world around him, saw its beauty, and wished to thank somebody for it. Maybe there were wells of love springing up from deep inside him, and he began by offering that love to God. The saddest thing about atheists is that, when they are feeling thankful for the good things in life, they do not know who to thank. Maybe Abel loved his brother too. God loves everything God has made, as we shall see in this story. But some people God also likes. Some people are more likeable than others. Abel was likeable, possibly good looking as well. Another possible meaning of his name has to do with its closeness to the Hebrew *Habil* meaning winsome or perhaps seductive. It occurs in the Song of Songs. Maybe Abel was 'a pretty boy' with something of the feminine about his looks and demeanour. Do we see portrayed in the behaviour of Cain the first example of homophobic aggression? People could get on with Abel. He was easy going, easy to please, good to chat with, interested in lots of things, interested in others.

What was wrong with Cain? Why wasn't he like Abel? He suffered by contrast with his younger brother. He had been born with a difficult personality. People with difficult personalities have to work hard with themselves. But if they do this effectively they can become extra special people, real treasures. They can be of help to others in ways that the easy going likeable person cannot. They can go deeper into things. God speaks to Cain in a loving parent sort of way. "Come on Cain, no need to pout like that. If you want to be accepted and liked, the answer lies with you. Just try being nice to people, get a smile on your face, you'll find it works wonders. Don't let that nasty little bug inside you get the better of you. Come on, you can do it. I'm here to help you."

If it was not homophobia, then the nasty little bug threatening to destroy Cain's chances of happiness was jealousy. Might have been both, of course. They are often connected. Jealousy is the only sin you can't enjoy, or so some say, perhaps with more experience than I have. Whenever I catch myself at it I slap my wrist. If ever you notice me slapping my wrist you'll know what's happening inside me. You have to nip jealousy in the bud. I have often been called upon to counsel people whose relationships were beginning to come apart. One of the biggest causes of failure in relationship is jealousy, unless it is pipped at the post by its ugly sister possessiveness. The two are dangerous because they are often mistaken for love, as in Shakespeare's tragedy Othello. Jealousy and possessiveness are not love; they are dark perversions.

Cain kills Abel. The editor of Genesis wants us to understand Cain as the archetypal murderer, in the same way as he wishes us to understand Adam as the archetypal human, and Adam with Eve as the archetypal opposite sex relationship. And the first thing we should note is that the first murderer was a man. Women can commit murders and they do. Women can be violent and they frequently are. Women can join the army and go to war, and these days they are represented in all the services. They can join in, even supervise the bullying of prisoners of war, as was shown on our television screens during the conflict in Iraq. It is an oversimplification to say that when a woman batters her husband, as happens more often than is generally realized or admitted, the couple are simply reversing gender roles. However, the statistics are clear – for once – that when it comes to one human killing another, or committing grievous bodily harm, so far in human history the men have outdone the women. There have to be prisons for women as well as for men, but so far we need less of them for women. So there appears to be in the male version of human a tendency to physical violence which is not so strong in the female version. This may be due to culture rather than nature. In many animal species the female is more deadly than the male. The bite of the female viper is more venomous than that of the male. And amongst many species of mammal the female will fight ferociously to the death for her young. Culture seems to play a larger role in the development of humans than in other species. It is no longer politically correct for a school teacher to say to her class, "I want four strong boys to help me move that table." The four strongest children in the class are liable to be two of the boys and two of the girls. However this sort of thing still goes on and is liable to do so for some time. The original teller of the story of Cain and Abel and the editor who uses the story in Genesis belong to the prevailing culture and have probably never heard of the Amazons. Cain is behaving like a man. God does not approve, but is not surprised – saw it coming in fact- and will be open to making allowances. God does not – please note Southern Baptists of the USA – call for the death penalty.

The second thing to note is that Cain murders Abel. Abel does not murder Cain. It is not a matter of Cain and Abel having a friendly fight with things getting out of hand, Cain proving the stronger or a better fighter than Abel. They were both strong men, of that we can be sure. Working the land and tending the flocks and herds both require practiced strength. Did Cain come at Abel from behind so that he had no chance to defend himself? Or was Cain's frontal attack such a surprise that Abel was caught off guard and a goner before he knew what was going on? Or was there a struggle, but Abel's heart was not in the fight whereas Cain was determined? He had certainly premeditated his crime. Since Cain means 'metal worker' it may be that this story is supposed also to account for the origin of weapons of war. Did Cain make the first spear? The name of the tribe Kenites also means metal workers, and they are found in Judges (1:16) near the copper mines in Egypt. Making weapons for the Egyptians?

The editor portrays two alternative types of manhood. Men who flex their muscles and regard aggression as a manly thing, and men who cherish their brothers and sisters. There is no doubt which God prefers. The portraits we are given are so very sketchy, and yet there is enough to draw conclusions as to the basic characters of the two brothers. God does not have to warn Abel about the misuse of his strength. There is no danger that Abel will murder Cain. Accidents can happen, but Abel is geared to the protection of his brother rather than his harm. In the Qur'an, Mohamed has Abel saying, *"If you raise your hand to kill me, I will not raise my hand to kill you."* Mohamed was familiar with the Hebrew scriptures, but it could be he received his account more directly from the Arab campfire tellers.

Cain's reply to God's enquiry concerning Abel's whereabouts, tells it all. "Am I my brother's keeper?" Yes, God expected that human beings would look after one another, even know where they were and the state of their welfare. Cain regarded another's fate as none of his business. That was his attitude. The editor is recounting the origins of humanity. He does not portray the first murder as simply a family matter, for according to his overall scheme, Cain and Abel are the human race in the making. In creating men and women, God had provided the opportunity for partnership and mutual care. And this was not just a programme for heterosexual relationships. God did not only create Adam and Eve. He also created Adam and Steve. They were supposed to care for one another too. The editor could have portrayed two sisters fighting and made the same point just as effectively. For the distinction is not between the sexes but a distinction common to the sexes, despite the provisional statistics that men are more prone to be violent than women. God did not create us to beat one another up, either physically, or mentally or emotionally. Aggression and violence are not God's plan. This is being made clear for us right at the beginning of the Bible, long before we get to the Israelites smiting the Amalakites and so on. The Israelites should have taken to heart this ancient camp fire story. Then they would not have made the mistake of thinking that God would tell them to do any such thing.

I thank my liberal evangelical father for insisting that scientific truth is from God just as much as the truth to be found in the Bible through diligent study. He taught me that evolution is common sense. "Look at your nails, my boy. They are the same as a monkey's!" However, some of the conclusions drawn from the facts of evolution have been transferred too readily into the realms of social and political thinking. The principle of 'The survival of the fittest' has been used to justify aggressive statecraft and economics, and educational systems that prepare nations for war. Animals need to be well fed and healthy in order to survive, but they do not have to be aggressive. I have two newspaper cuttings on my wall. One is about a Japanese rat snake who feeds on rodents, but when given a live hamster refused to eat it. Instead he adopted it as its bosom pal. The other is of an abandoned baby boy in Argentina who was looked after, protected, kept clean and fed by a group of wild cats. It is in the nature of humankind – it should be obvious – to care for other humans and for other living species, as it is in the nature of other living species to care for one another and even for us. This caring instinct must surely play a role in the survival of species. Some would no doubt label the instinct as 'maternal'. But what is meant by that? It is not only mothers who care. I saw on a BBC nature watch program a whole family of choughs being reared single-handed by the father bird after the mother had been killed in an accident. The biologists watching calculated it would not be possible for the father to have all the time and energy to make sufficient journeys to and fro the nest to feed the chicks. They were doomed. But the father did it, and they all survived! Yes, he had to be fit. But he also had to care! The dedication of those people working hard to protect endangered species, is it just a quirk? Or is it part of human nature, and essential to all sentient beings?

If the world of living beings is to survive, it will only do so if the caring instinct of Abel overcomes the aggressive instinct of Cain. That means not only that the Abels must be encouraged, rather than be thought of as sissies or wimps. The Cains must listen to the voice of God without and within and seek to become more like Abel. Abels must resist the Macho culture that seeks to make them more like Cain. Aggression still rules in politics. The most chilling words I have ever heard from a Prime Minister in my life time are those from Tony Blair, "We are a nation that goes to war." Alas he was telling the truth for once. Next to the USA our country devotes a greater proportion of its GNP to defence than any other nation on earth. Our economy depends on the arms industry. We even sell arms to potential enemies. There is an in-built majority in the population of the British Isles (though perhaps it is only England) that will support a war enthusiastically, whatever the circumstances, whatever the pretext , whatever the political colour of the government. British statesmen can confidently take the country to war, knowing this will be the case. There will also be a highly vocal and active minority against most wars, but these are no more than an irritant and can be ignored. After the Suez War, the Conservative government was re-elected; similarly after the Falklands War, triumphantly. The Labour Government was re-elected after it had taken the country into the wars in Iraq and Afghanistan.

Aggression also rules religion today. There was a strong streak of desire for a crusade against Islam in the Iraq war as Rowan Williams pointed out at the time in his book 'Writing in the Dust'. He was nearby in New York at the time of the attack on the twin towers. Fundamentalism whether Muslim, Jewish or Christian (Protestant or Catholic) is potentially violent. It is intolerant in belief and ruthless in method, and frequently allies itself with oppressive regimes.

So it's an uphill task. The Church, as well as the world has to be educated out of the macho and into the luvo. Let there be peace on earth and let it begin with me. We have to deal with the Cain in us and encourage the Abel.

The second part of the story has to do with Cain's fate after the murder of Abel. God does not hand out the death penalty. Instead Cain is sentenced to hard labor. If the story teller were telling the story today, he or she might say community service rather than hard labor. Or Cain is to be an asylum seeker. It is difficult to reconcile these two penalties. Maybe there were two versions of the same story. Cain is also to have a taste of his own medicine. He will know what it is like to be on the receiving end of others' aggression towards *him*. This smacks of modern techniques of reforming criminals by encouraging them to face up to their crimes, sometimes by meeting their victims and getting victimizer to imagine what it feels like to be in the victim's shoes. However, God is not in favor of humans taking the law into their own hands and organizing vigilantes. God is the one responsible for the righting of wrongs. If they lay a finger on Cain, then God will put them on community service too – seven times the amount put on Cain. (Seven is usually a symbolic number in scripture. Here it just means 'a harder sentence'.) This all shows us clearly that the original story of Cain and Abel was not attached to the story of Adam and Eve. There were plenty of people about to cause grief to Cain, who were obviously not all descendents of Cain's father. Cain is to wander from one country to another and meet people everywhere he goes. These will recognize Cain, or distinguish themselves from him, because there will be something distinctive about him. Your guess as to what this was is as good as mine. Perhaps one of his fellow metal workers branded him, a primitive sort of tattoo. Mr. Macho again – he could take the pain! Or maybe he was a black man and the Garden of Eden from which he fled was East Africa where anthropologists believe we all began. Perhaps he was the first victim of colour prejudice. Some believe that Cain had ginger hair and that the Kenites were all ginger headed. Ginger headed people are bullied sometimes. The ancient Celtic shamans who still survive in these islands believe that all red heads are psychic, though many suppress their skills.

Whatever was 'different' about Cain, God is Cain's protector. God was on the side of Abel when Abel was a victim of violence. God is on the side of Cain when Cain is the victim. Whatever the 'Mark of Cain', whether black skin, red hair or whatever, it is miscalled, for it is 'God's Mark', the sign of God's ownership. Those who suffer rejection and abuse because they are different are under God's guardianship. However strong they may be physically, they are the 'little ones' Jesus tells us not to despise. (Matthew 18:10) Soldiers in their uniforms are not to be despised. Those who shout cat-calls at them are not people of peace. Soldiers are not only schooled in violence, arguably victimization. They are also victims of violence. Often if they survive the conflict, they are the victims of their employers' ingratitude and neglect, as well as having long-lasting psychological problems and social disorientation. Some end up in prison.

The story ends with bad news and good news. Cain settles in the land of 'Nod' a word that means 'wandering'. He settles, but is unsettled. A tortured soul, perhaps to the end of his days. How could he ever forgive himself for killing his brother? Our societies are keen on punishing criminals. It never seems to occur to some people that some criminals punish themselves much harder than anyone else could punish them. The punishment Cain inflicts on himself is to 'go from the presence of God'. Does he also become the world's first atheist? What a lot goes on in this one person! To choose to live as if there is no God, to convince yourself there is no such being as God, despite all the evidence within you and around you, must be a very difficult and psychologically painful thing to do. I find happy atheists rare. I suppose they must be around in their millions somewhere, but I find them hard to find. In the days of Stalin when the state attempted to enforce atheism on the whole population, the whole Russian people seemed to go around with sullen looks on their faces. They certainly didn't look liberated from anything. However atheists may protest, atheism is life without hope, here in this life and in whatever life there is to come.

Cain tries to get away from God. But he cannot. God has put God's mark upon him. He belongs to God, God is his friend, even though that may seem impossible to him. So let's take this on board. God is not just the God of Abel, who is celebrated as the first martyr – the first death of a righteous and Christlike man before Christ. God is also the God of Cain, the bounder, the failure, the miserable outcast from respectable society. God is God of the atheist. Even atheists have God's mark on them. God can speak through the atheist, frequently does – through Stephen Hawking, Richard Dawkins, Christopher Hitchens, Philip Pullman. They offer God's truth to the Church. They offer essential criticism the Church is not able or willing to give itself. Cain may have left God; God has not left Cain; Cain has God's mark. Neither is God just the God of 'modern man', the man in touch with his feminine side. God is also God of Mr. Macho, and loves those flexing muscles. Just use those arms for hugging, for carrying the loads, for lifting the weights, for protecting the weak. That's all God asks.

The good news is that Cain finds a wife. He finds a companion and we wonder and we hope it made up in some measure for the loss of his brother. And wow they had a son called Enoch. Was this the same Enoch who walked with God? The genealogies are very muddled and confusing and come from many sources. We cannot be literalist about them. Although there seem to be two different Enochs in the lists, they may be the same one. The atheist bears a son who is hyper God conscious? So, so possible. Cain and Carrie may well be the ancestors of Jethro the priest of Midian who shares his experience of God with Moses. Moses married Zipporah, Jethro's daughter. Did she have red hair?

The older I get and the longer the life I have to look back on, the more I am aware of God having a plan A, a plan B, a plan C … and so on down the line. God is the great adaptable one. Not only is God the 'God of surprises', but God is ready and open to surprises and willing to respond accordingly. According to the poem in Genesis chapter 1, the whole created universe was a surprise to God – a good one! Each step in the process of evolution was a new and joyful experience for God. That's the impression the poet gives. God does not have everything wrapped up from beginning to end as many pious people believe. What a boring old fart some people turn God into! According to the camp-fire stories, God did not always will or anticipate the way things turned out. God did not want Cain to murder Abel so that Abel's physical line would come to an end. God did not want Cain to become a frightened recluse. That's what happened, so God went on to plan B or plan C. God's love line that seemed to come to an end in the death of Abel is carried forward in Cain.

Come, Christian friends there's plenty here for all to do;
God will supply the tools you need and give the know-how too.
With God the weak are strong, the over cautious dare.
Eagerly venture with a song and gladly burdens share!

2) Enjoy the Spirit's harvest – patience, joy and peace;
As you express and practice love, it surely will increase;
Loyalty, gentleness and generosity,
Kindness and self control – all serve to set the closed mind free.

3) Don't seek the bully's prize or power's security;
Don't sit with those who judge, or spread around guilt's misery;
Join with the victimized and be the outcast's friend;
Then you'll be one with Christ, tired and content at work
day's end.

(John Henson. After Charles Wesley –
'Soldiers of Christ arise' Tune:
'From strength to strength')

CHAPTER SEVEN

NOAH, HAM AND NUDITY.
'NUDITY NOT PRUDERY'.

Although in the early years of our marriage we were 'strapped' for money, Valerie and I decided that our children should have at least one quality toy, and that meant a Noah's Ark, made by 'Good Wood' from Hamley's catalogue. For well over 100 years, this children's toy had been popular among the pious middle classes, chiefly because it depicted a Biblical story, and might therefore be played with even on Sunday. No one ever questioned whether the story was a suitable one for children. Lining the animals up in twos, learning their names, and parading them into the Ark was probably as far as most young children got with the story. Older children were told the unquestioned truth that if people were naughty, God had some very unpleasant ways of dealing with them. Our Noah's

Ark still exists, rather worn, but the toy is no longer popular, and its story now makes everyone uncomfortable, religious and irreligious alike. Many Christians can no longer accept the view of God the story portrays. On the other hand, with the advent of Climate Change, already taking place, are the dire consequences of those who do not take the warnings of prophets speaking today. They speak on behalf of science rather than God. The story has a scary resonance for those suffering drought in California and those in Bangladesh who watch their whole country going beneath the waters before their eyes. It also has inspiration for those who are endeavouring to rescue endangered species.

Predictably, there are still those who believe the Biblical story word for word. You can see in northern Turkey on Mount Ararat, not the Ark but a large stone which kept the Ark in balance while on the stormy seas. There is a visitors centre and souvenir shop, of course. In 1937 one Ron Wyatt found what appear to be the outlines of a large boat on a slope near Ararat. A photo was taken from a plane in 1959 and there have been radar scans. However, geologists say that there are geological explanations for the strange shapes. You pays your money and…

As a historian I have to ask what historical truth there is likely to be in the story. There are flood stories in many cultures around the world, including Greece, Babylon and India. That is because throughout history and pre-history there have been many big floods, and no doubt remarkable examples of survival against the odds. The survivors would have handed down the stories to their descendants, because without their exceptional luck, those descendants would have never been. As to the particular flood in Genesis, the two most possible sites for the flood historically would seem to be either Mesopotamia, the land of the two rivers, which often flood, but whose waters might have been augmented with a tidal wave up the Persian Gulf. Or – and this is the explanation I prefer – the flood story may record the making of the Black Sea when a combination of raised water levels in the Mediterranean, the wearing away of the rocks which formed a barrier to land below sea level, suddenly led to a massive rush of water into what then became a big extension of the Mediterranean to provide a coastline for eastern Europe, Russia and Turkey. Ararat is not far away in northern Turkey. Anyone who possessed a boat would obviously have had an advantage, and some might even have been able to save not only themselves, but some of their livestock. It does not require much imagination to see how one story could have been embroidered over and over, and then given a theological twist, to become the Noah story.

In the first three chapters of Genesis we see the God of creation making changes day by day. This God is experimenting in freedom, and the message of Noah's story in chapters seven to nine is that the experiment continues. It is an experiment with sex, which is shown to be dangerous and unpredictable, but also dynamic, beautiful, creative and funny.

On my holiday in June 2015 at the home of my cousin Jean who lives in Crete, I set myself to watch the controversial film 'Noah'. I don't know whether to call the film horrible or horrifying, but I will settle for both, at least it was to my sensitivities. I am generally not into horror. I was not horrified, as some were bound to be, by the Biblical inaccuracies. But I believe the portrayal of the story to be more true to the Bible than literal 'Bible-Believer' accounts, simply because of the unmitigated horror for most of the film. Pious literalistic readers manage to fit the story into their understanding of God's justice, which means that they take lightly the mass slaughter of humankind, men, women, children plus all other land animals. To them if God thinks people worthy of such a fate, then so they are. The film makes sure the viewer does not escape the intensity of the horror of the flood itself but also the effect on the minds and personalities of those who we are to take as God's special friends, the family of Noah. The portrayal here is of a horrible, monstrous God, who decides to wipe out all living things because his experiment with the earth has not been successful. He (for it is surely 'he'), is utterly ruthless and totally without mercy – even does a preliminary Sodom and Gomorrah act by fire on one lot of humans (in the wrong place Biblically) before the big one with water. Unimpressed by the fundamentalists' assurance that 'God always knows best' , my mind says that if God had had one jot of sympathy in him, he could just have gently put the race of humankind permanently to sleep with a divine anaesthetic. (As he did temporally with the help of Noah on the animals in this version of the parable.) What need of such terror and torture except to satisfy the lusts of a hyper-sadist? And as for the pious and righteous Noah, his Godliness consists entirely of doing whatever he thinks God wants him to do, irrespective of what pain he causes, including the contemplation of killing his own baby granddaughters to prevent the human race from surviving. Unlike God , he seems to have some pacifist misgivings. He is a vegetarian and will not pick a wild flower for fear of harm to the environment. Yet when push comes to shove he can adopt violence to fend off his opponents. Neither he, nor his God, come over as any better than the humans they are determined to liquidate. But this could be central to the meaning of the parable, or of the parable as we should understand it today.

We should take our cue from the ace teller of parables – Jesus. Jesus told stories in order to stimulate questions in the minds of the hearers. Those who look for a fixed or literalist interpretation of Jesus' parables miss the point of his customary parting shot – "If you've got ears, use them!" Jesus' stories are not literal truth. They are 'WHAT IF STORIES'. What if Jews and Samaritans (or Palestinians) had a care for one another as did the good man in the story? What would the world be like then? What would family and community relationships be like if parents and siblings forgave one another as the father did in the story of the Adventurous Son? What would politics and society be like if the first were last and the last were first? And to apply the principle to the Noah story, "Would it really work if God just scrapped the lot and started all over again every time things got out of hand?" Of course it wouldn't.

The incident of Noah discovering the potency of fermented grapes, becoming drunk and besporting himself naked is very lightly done in the film, and those who have never read the Bible story might wonder what is going on in the film version or miss it altogether. Far from being the father of a new, cleansed human race, Noah becomes a prey to the demon drink.

The climax of the story of Noah is not the pretty rainbow, declaring God's ceasing of hostilities as he directs the arrows towards himself, and declares with a splash of colour a preference for variety. The climax is the incident between the drunken and perhaps sexually frisky Noah, his youngest son Ham, and his two brothers. It is clear evidence that God's experiment with the flood has not worked. Ham is a key character in the film. He is a rebel, and his rebelliousness has in part to do with the authoritarian and patriarchal attitudes of his father. 'Daddy knows best'. Ham falls in love with one of the humans destined for the chop. He also loves her family and friends. This indiscriminate love thing is infectious and has to stop! He is disobedient and stroppy with his father Noah, and even falls for a time into the hands of Tubal Cain, who is a survivor of the old wickedness, exampled by his taste for meat. He tried to get Ham to be 'a man' by killing his own father. Ham ends up killing Tubal Cain instead, which pleases Tuba Cain because he thinks that at least he has succeeded in making Ham a man. But Ham's killing of Tubal Cain is rather an expression of his love for Noah – that awkward, unruly emotion again.

In the film we only see Noah getting drunk on his rotting grapes and lying in the distance on the beach. We can hardly see that he has no clothes on. We see, but do not hear, a short conversation between Ham and his brothers. Then the two brothers go and cover Noah up, while Ham stands at a distance, not knowing quite what to make of their behaviour. The Biblical account is more explicit. Noah is lying in his tent naked. (A private enough place, one would have thought.) By accident Ham goes into the tent and sees him. Perhaps his gaze lingers. (Typically Michael Angelo painted the scene giving Noah a huge erection.) The fundamentalists have their own interpretation of this. It is obviously a wicked thing for a man to 'behold his father's nakedness' as the KJV coyly puts it. Thus at the times of the controversy over the abolition of slavery, equal rights in the USA and apartheid in South Africa, fundamentalists argued that the African races were inferior, cursed by God, because they were descendents of the horrible Ham who did that awful sinful thing.

But the whole exercise of the Flood was supposed to be a return to Eden before the fall. If that's the case, then a return to a more relaxed attitude to nakedness should surely be a positive rather than a negative consequence. Surely here no sexual offence was committed by either Noah or Ham. The offenders were the two brothers with their self-righteous, prudish and unreasonable condemnation.

The film gets it right. Ham departs from his dysfunctional family to seek his own fortune, expressing the hope that one day the world will be a kinder place. Thus it is Ham not Noah who emerges as the hero and ideal human of this story. And it is to Ham's spiritual descendents the world must look in hope.

In this story Ham represents the 'Love Line'. "Splendid are the gentle: the world will be safe in their hands." (Matthew 5. GOOD AS NEW)

In an article entitled 'Naturism and Christian Belief' (1980) my friend Adrian Thatcher *argued the case for consenting groups of people to take all their clothes off and to spend life living naturally without shame or fear. (Daring for those days.) He writes:

*"The case for naturism, and for having a joyful and un-hung attitude to the body and to sex generally, is overwhelmingly made out by the Bible itself, but has long been overlooked by stuffy interpreters, who couldn't draw the obvious conclusions from what they read. In one of the creations stories, when the Lord God made Man and Woman, 'they were both naked', the man and his wife, 'but they had no feeling of shame towards one another'. (Gen. 2:25 New English Bible). Only later after they both eat the forbidden fruit do they get hung up about feeling naked and cover up with fig leaves. (Gen. 3:7) In the myth going around starkers is God's will. He intended it. The need to cover up only arises **out of wrong attitudes**. Even then, they only wear 'loincloths'. The age of the bikini was still a long way off."*

I would add to this sound interpretation of the Genesis parable, that the 'original pair' commit two sins. (Actually Adam and Eve represent all humankind, and not a denial of evolution, which in any case the opening poem in Genesis 1 seems to describe). The first sin is to eat something a parent has forbidden – and what child has never done that? Easily put right – admit it; say sorry; be forgiven. The second is much more serious. The pair 'hide from God' so that God has to call out "Adam, where are you?" It is their hiding from God that grieves God's heart, and makes relationship difficult, especially hiding their most intimate body parts which God had taken great trouble to create, beautiful and good, as every other part of the human body. Imagine what Sir Christopher Wren would have thought if the dome of St. Paul's Cathedral got covered up because it looked like a breast? 'Hiding from God' is of course intended to be understood as symbolizing every other kind of pretence, hypocrisy and prudery. As Jesus suggested to the Pharisees, "Just because you turn your heads away to avoid looking at a woman, it doesn't mean you are not getting all steamed up inside."

I saw a re-enactment of the Noah story by means of a video on Facebook. A beautiful and exceedingly athletic young man gate-crashed one of those commando course sporting features competitors go through, up and down, under and over all sorts of equipment as fast as they can to prove their prowess. This young man appeared from nowhere and went through the whole lot at top speed, putting all other competitors to shame, and he was completely naked. He went so fast that no one could catch him, and with such skill that every nook and cranny of his anatomy was completely revealed. But in the video we were shown – as per 'normal' USA practice- mysterious clouds covered up the offending parts throughout. If it had happened in most parts of Europe (except the British Isles) viewers would have been considered adult enough to see the lot. "What about the children?" I hear you squeal. The children are not the problem!

I saw a glimpse of Eden regained on a visit to the Dominican Republic and the capital San Domingo. A friend and I were sitting on the promenade over-looking the beach towards the end of the afternoon, when a couple of dozen or more black young men in their teens and early twenties appeared running the length of the beach and then playing games, all completely naked. There were many people walking along the prom. No-one apart from ourselves took any notice. It probably happened every day. It was a truly beautiful and exhilarating sight. The descendents of Ham were enjoying the freedom of their naked bodies, just as God intended.

So I would say that the last episode of the parable of Noah has been infamously misinterpreted. It is not about the sin of being naked to the sight of others. It is a story about the tragic results of prudery. It was not Ham, but Shem and Japheth who postponed Paradise regained, providing racism with an additional raison d'être. Yes, humanity has another chance. There is always another chance with God.

[* Dr. Adrian Thatcher is Professor Emeritus of Theology in the University of Exeter (England) and author of many progressive Christian books, including 'God, Sex and Gender'.]

Noah saw the bright rainbow

Noah saw the bright rainbow;
It was good to see;
Taught him that the Loving God
Likes variety.

Ancient poets taught that God
Made the world in days;
Full of many kinds of life,
Singing out God's praise.

Though we see things different now;
We can still adore;
Wonder at diversity,
There is always more.

Jacob gave his son a dress;
Joseph he was called,
Colours fit for a princess;
Some thought it too bold.

Jesus contemplated flowers
Yellow, pink and blue;
God cares for them every one;
We should prize them too.

Once a seer imagined heaven;
Stones of every hue;
Rainbow round the golden throne;
There's a place for you.

So if we are straight or gay,
Maybe queerer still;
We can value everyone,
As God always will.

John Henson
(Dedicated to Peterson and Glen.)

Chapter Eight

More Naked
in the Bible.

What God shows Moses
(Exodus 33: 17-23)

Many of the stories that were collected to make up the first 5 books
of the Bible come from very primitive times. In context they were
so presented as to lessen the primitive elements and express more
lofty understandings of the divine. Down the ages theologians
have continued this process by interpreting the stories as they now
stand to produce even more civilized and sophisticated spiritual
lessons for their readers. But frequently little sparks of the primitive
may still be seen. This snippet from Exodus is a good example.

Moses is trying to make friends with God. To make a friend
you must discover as much about them as possible, preferably

with their cooperation. But to Moses God appears rather coy. God has divulged his/her (how can Moses be sure?) name. The name is 'I am' or rather 'I am what I am', which does not tell Moses very much except that God is mysterious. Moses is not satisfied. He wants to know all about his new friend. Just like a Facebook user Moses needs more than a name – he wants an address, details of hobbies and interests, and most of all a picture "Show me your glory", Moses says. He wants to know what God looks like. (v.18) God reminds Moses of the old wives' tale 'You cannot see God's face and live'. (v20) But God is at his most playful today. God gets Moses to stand or crouch behind a rock where, without a pair of specs not yet invented, Moses will only get a limited view – a bit like the cheapest seats in a theatre. Then God appears, facing away from Moses. God uses a hand as a shield, and then removes it, and for a split second Moses gets a glimpse of God's bottom. It's hilarious, and if only theologians were capable of sharing God's sense of humour, they would actually learn a lot. They would be able to understand many of the difficult things Jesus said.

The bottom tends to be included together with breasts (female ones) and genitals as parts of the body that in western society we are supposed to be ashamed of, and not look at in respect of other peoples'. 'Mooning' – pulling down the trousers, bending over and exposing the bare bottom is a form of insult, even used by cheeky miners at the time of the miners' strike to insult the police, and by the Scottish army in 'Braveheart' to put fear into the hearts of the English.

But exposing those parts of the body not often seen can also be a mark of friendship or comradeship. It is usually taken for granted within marriage, and also among members of sports teams or military units. God may have been teasing Moses, but he was not insulting him. He was deepening the friendship, and whatever you think of this interpretation, friendship was what was happening between God and Moses. We now know that God offers friendship to all. But it is not something you can just walk into without a 'by your leave'. Friendship with God takes time and a learning curve, like every true friendship. "I am his and he is mine". Oh no you're not. You've only just started.

To tie this story in with the stories of Eden and Noah, we must say that if God was happy to see Adam and Eve in the noddy and Noah too, God would not be unwilling to appear in the noddy.

[I am grateful to my college Principal, Dr. Henton Davies, a distinguished Hebrew scholar, for the suggestion that 'back' in the text may be a euphemism for 'backside'.]

DAVID'S DANCE
(2 SAMUEL 6: V16 & 20-21)

King David was one of the four great heroes of the Israelite people, together with Abraham, Moses and Elijah. If Abraham represents the ancient tradition, Moses the legal structure, Elijah the voice of prophetic protest, then David represents charisma. David was ever keen and colourful. He was capable of enlisting fierce loyalties; he was a gifted entertainer, a poet and musician, and it was these gifts that first led him to be introduced to the court of King Saul David had a special gift for friendship, eliciting the undying love of others; and above all, like Abraham, Moses and Elijah, he was possessed of a religious genius and close mates with God.

Proof of David's religious genius was bringing together the traditional worship of Yahweh (= I AM) with that of the Jebusite Jerusalem where El Elyon (=God Most High) was worshipped. To symbolize this David brought the Ark in procession to Jerusalem. The Ark was a gold-layered wooden box, which served both as I AM's throne when stationary and I AM's chariot when moving. (The folks in those days did not make the same distinction between the symbolic and the actual that we make, and they would not have understood it.) So on this occasion I AM was in his chariot and David was in front, putting on an extra special entertainment for the deity. David was never one to do things by halves. He danced and performed acrobatics, cartwheels and the like. And he was dressed only in an ephod. The closest thing we have to what David was wearing today is probably our T-shirt, except that the ephod was looser so that when David did a summersault his flimsy costume would fly over his head, revealing all. David kept up his act all the way to the gates of the city and to the holy shrine. He was accompanied by a group of female dancers, servant girls from his court. I AM, in his chariot, had the grandstand view. Someone else with a good view was his wife Michelle who was looking out through an upstairs window. She was appalled. Her husband had exposed his intimate parts to all and sundry. King or no king, Michelle told David just what she thought of him. "How the King of Israel honoured himself today, uncovering himself before the eyes of his servant maids , as any vulgar fellow might shamelessly uncover himself!" David had been flashing. It seems to have been the end of the marriage between David and Michelle. David's reply did not convince his wife. But the scripture writer wishes us to be convinced of David's sincerity. "I was dancing for God." God was his friend, his most intimate friend, and he had put on his best show. He had not made the same mistake as Adam and Eve. He had appeared before God without a fig leaf.

Izzy bares all
(Isaiah chapter 20)

The sense of joy and liberation that David expressed in his uninhibited dancing and self-display in the presence of his God reflects a time in the history of the Israelite peoples which they looked back on with a mixture of pride and nostalgia. It was when their united tribes experienced peace and prosperity for the most part. The next time one of God's friends felt impelled to be so daring, the times were very different. The separated kingdom of the northern ten tribes had been destroyed by Assyria, and their people taken into exile or dispersed. The tiny kingdom of Judah now looked next in line for destruction, and its politicians were seeking an alliance with Egypt and Ethiopia. Izzy, previous priest and courtier, spoke in the name of God. He called the nation to trust and not to do anything to provoke the enemy. Like most prophets he was ignored. So Izzy decided that desperate measures were needed. He would go to extremes in an act of prophetic symbolism. There was no T.V., no films, no books with coloured pictures in those days. And since Izzy had failed to engage the imagination of the people by his lyrics sung to the accompaniment of his primitive guitar, he decided to be more dramatic. He stripped naked and walked the streets in that condition for three years. He was not arrested for indecency. (This was not the UK or the USA.) But we do not know whether he got his point across. He was asking his people to imagine what was going to happen to the Egyptian captives when they were taken by the Assyrians. They might very well pass near to Judah on their way to exile in Assyria, naked and humiliated, with – worst of all – their buttocks exposed, just like animals. And that is what it would be like with the people of Judah if they did not show more sense. There was nothing joyful or entertaining about Izzy's bare bottom. It was intended to provoke fear and reflection. But Izzy was at one with David in this: If being God's friend meant stripping off naked in public, God could count on him!

MARK

(MARK 14: 51-52. SEE ALSO 14:13-15 & 16: 5-7)

Mark in his account of the 'Good News' of Jesus, shows us that he was an essential eye witness to some of the events he records, not just a recorder of stories told to him by others. He was witness and participant in the three key events at the end of the gospel story – the communion meal in the 'Upper Room' (most likely the function room in the hotel owned by Mark's parents) ; the Passion, which began in the garden on Olive Hill; and the empty grave marking Jesus' return from death. Three autobiographical cameos – the mystic number.

Mark's presence in the secret meeting spot near the old olive press was crucial, as it turned out. What was he doing there, and what was he doing there naked apart from a flimsy white sheet with no belt to hold it in place? We shall never really know. (For a re-construction more or less on conventional lines see the chapters 'The Gethsemane Streaker' in my book 'The Gay Disciple.) What is certain is that Mark created a diversion at a critical point. Jesus had been arrested and someone (probably Rocky) was just about to be arrested for offering resistance with a weapon. But a glimpse was caught of Mark's white attire, clear in the light of the burning torches. The mob was distracted and joined in a chase after Mark, allowing Rocky, Thunder and Lightning to scarper. One of the pursuers managed to grab hold of Mark's sheet, but Mark let go and ran off naked. He was some way from home and would have to get there with nothing on. It was dark, but Jerusalem was a busy city with a night life, so it must have been a bit tricky. The intriguing question is, did someone in the garden catch a glimpse of him out of the corner of their eye, or did Mark deliberately cause the distraction? In either case, he may well have saved one or even all three of Jesus' companions from arrest. The Good Friday story would have been quite different. Perhaps Mark is trying to say something more deeply spiritual. He ran away from the concentration of evil that had the upper hand in Gethsemane. In so doing he lost his clothes. Baptism in the early church was marked by setting aside the garments in which you approached the pool of water, and the putting on of new clothes after your dipping. Perhaps this experience of nakedness and the loss of the old was the turning point for Mark spiritually. Freedom to cast aside the old, freedom to count himself a friend of Jesus, freedom to be Adam as he was intended to be before he hid in shame from God, and freedom to live a new life without guilt or fear.

It was also probably Mark who had been the chap who showed Jesus' friends the way to the hotel, which must have been tucked away in a back street somewhere, because it was difficult to find. He was doing a woman's job carrying a pitcher of water, and Peterson Toscano portrays him as wearing woman's apparel. Certainly he seemed to have an eccentric taste in clothing. He may have been transgender or had transvestite tendencies. But Mark is telling us that before his part in the Passion, he had a part to play in the Thursday night communion. It was he who had provided the water that would be on the table with the wine, and maybe also the water with which Jesus washed his friends' feet. Maybe Mark was present as a member of the hotel owners' family and had his feet washed by Jesus too.

In his third cameo, Mark describes himself as the very first visitor to Jesus' grave – the cave hewn out of the rock, which was now open and empty. Again his clothes were eye-catching. The Greek word may mean white or bright. They shone in the light of the morning. The new man was wearing his new clothes. They must have been something startling. The impact they caused on the women sent them away screaming in fear. "Hey, come back! Nothing to be afraid of. It's me, John Mark, from the hotel!" In Matthew's gospel Mark becomes an 'angel'. The word angel means 'messenger'. Mark was the first messenger, as he was probably also the first gospel-writer, to announce Jesus' Resurrection.

ROCKY

Rocky does not get a good press in the gospels. His name was a nickname given to him by Jesus. The name carried with it more than a tinge of Jewish leg-pulling. 'Peter' means nothing in English other than a popular first name. The French are more fortunate. Pierre means a 'stone'. For Jesus describes not the rock upon which a builder should build (petra), but the sort of large rock or stone you could pick up if you are very strong. It was the sort of rock that could be used in a Roman catapult and be projected towards the walls or gate of a fortress, but also if you stood on it would rock (petros). Rocky was an unreliable character. This he coupled with proud boasting. He thought he was up to walking on water like Jesus, but when he tried he missed his footing on the stepping stones and fell in. Jesus had to fish him out. He had to be told that forgiveness is an on-going process, not a one-off event. But he forgot all that in the case of Nye and Sapphire (Acts 5). Most notoriously of all he denied having ever setting eyes on Jesus three times, despite having confidently asserted that he would do no such thing. The others might – but not him! That was not the 'sin' of which Jesus sought to remind him on the lakeside in Galilee. Jesus always has compassion and understanding with regard to failures. Rocky's problem was that he wanted to be Mr. Macho, and he wasn't. According to the 'Quo Vadis' legend, that remained his problem to the end of his life. The crucified and risen Jesus met him on the road running away from the persecution in Rome. "Where are you going, Leader?" "I am going to Rome to be crucified again!"

The story of the communion on the beach after a large catch of fish is told in the last chapter of 'Sources Close to Jesus.' The whole chapter is packed with symbolism and innuendo. That includes the humorous incident where Rocky, realizing it is Jesus on the beach, grabs his clothes before jumping into the water. Most people take their clothes off to go into the sea, but Rocky puts them on! Fishing naked with his pals was something Rocky probably did frequently in the warm weather. But meeting the leader, who he had recently let down, without a stitch on, was something he couldn't face. We are back with Adam and Eve covering themselves up when they felt guilty. Jesus is not concerned about Rocky telling lies in the High Priest's courtyard. But he is concerned about Rocky's unwillingness to face up to himself. Today Jesus might suggest he did a Myers Briggs. "Do you love me?", Jesus asks – an embarrassing question to a He-man, the man who had made a fuss over Jesus wanting to wash his feet. Jesus now calls him by his real name, Simon Johnson. "Let's forget about being that hard stone for a moment, Simon. Let's talk about your feelings. Someone told me you cried when you ran out of courtyard. Was that love for me, or annoyance with yourself?" "And what was all that about, putting your clothes on to come to meet me? They are still soaking wet. Anyone would think I'd never seen your cock before. Get real man! In the soldiers' torture room , and on the cross I went naked for you and for the world. Naked I was born and I died naked too." But I'm calling you to follow me, to look after all those other sheep and lambs who are as weak as you are. And if you do that you will end up being crucified, naked like me, for that is the Roman way." (The tradition is that Rocky returned to Rome and was crucified upside-down. But every Church tradition should be accompanied by a warning. They may be untrue.)

God knows what we look like, both physically and spiritually. We may hide from one another, but there is no hiding from God. And we should not try to hide – from God, from others, or from ourselves.

Finally some words of Jesus from the Gospel of Thomas (GAN 'Thought-Provoking Sayings of Jesus, extracts from chapters 1&2) Just to think about, or as Jesus would say, "If you've got ears, use them!"

Maggie asked Jesus, "What sort of people do you want your friends to be?" Jesus told a story. "One day some children were innocently playing in a field. The farmer came along and said, "This is my field, get out of it!" The children stripped in front of the farmer to show they had stolen nothing and said, 'You can have your field, we mean you no harm!' "

One day Jesus saw some mothers feeding their babies at the breast. Jesus said to his friends, "Little babies are the perfect example for those who want to be citizens of God's New World." The friends said, "Surely we don't have to become babies in order to qualify for the New World?" Jesus replied, "When two people become one, like a mother feeding her child; when there's no difference between the way you behave and what's going on in your mind, or between your head and your heart; when you treat males and females equally, without any distinctions whatsoever; when you respond naturally to another's body language; when you accept people as they are, – then you'll be ready for God's New World."

Jesus said, "When you learn to be like little children who, without feeling the least bit shy, take off all their clothes and leave them in an untidy heap on the floor, then you'll relate to God's True Likeness without embarrassment."

Sayings of Jesus, Gospel of Thomas
– page 69 para 2 & para 5; & pg 71
GOOD AS NEW)

The Sauna

(In memory of the Empire Pool Turkish Baths of Cardiff)

I like going to the Sauna;
There I exile myself from the courts of Zion,
Though some of Zion's children are usually there – incognito.
In the Sauna I meet the other refugees from the world-
taxcollectors and Pharisees, lawyers and street sweepers,
prostitutes and social workers, opera singers and artists,
(I once met Wayne Sleep, and we talked about Jesus)
saints and sinners – more saints than you would imagine.
They are all there, made one by their nakedness – no, not quite.
Fat and thin, smooth and hairy, old and not old yet,
beautiful friendly, and beautiful untouchable,
bold and timid, silent and talkative.
black, white, Arab, Asian,
Christian, Jew, Moslem, Hindu, Buddhist, Shaman, Atheist,
Agnostic.
God goes with me everywhere, so comes to the sauna,
though is there already.
Some think I bring God in – they are wrong,
They do!

I return to the courts of Zion, where I also belong.
There I talk a lot.
But I do not talk about the sauna.

(John Henson 2/3/2016)

CHAPTER NINE

LONG-SUFFERING WOMEN

ZIPPY
(EXODUS 4: 24-26)

Moses was on his way back to Egypt to perform the task God had assigned to him, to release the Hebrew slaves from their cruel Egyptian masters. Moses was not at all happy about this job. He had told God that he was not up to it over and over again until his nerves were in tatters, and even when God told him that his handsome, smooth-tongued brother Aaron could do all the talking, he didn't feel any better about it. His wife Zippy was no help. She nagged him all the way, making it clear that she thought it a hare-brained idea. Their two little boys Gershom and Eliezer were also a pain. Zippy had no control over them, and Moses thought it would have been better if they had been left back at home with his father-in-law Jethro, who stood no nonsense. By the time Moses had set up their tent ready to bed down for the night, he was troubled by pains in his belly. His bowels were not working. He had not been able to relieve himself in the bushes for some time and was having difficulty in passing water. Soon after he had laid down with Zippy by his side with the two boys just about asleep at his feet, he suddenly let out a wild scream. He was in agony. He knew what this must be, of course. What had he done to displease God this time? Everyone knew that whenever you suffered, even the slightest twinge, it was your god punishing you for your sin. What other explanation could there be? God enjoyed doing this, and even punished you for sins you had committed when you could not think for the life of you what you had done wrong. Only one thing for it. Moses would have to make a sacrifice. The only way a god could be appeased was by seeing blood being shed. But they had no animals with them. Even if he felt up to hunting, there was no game in this part of the desert, none that the great 'I AM' would fancy, anyway. I AM thought that snakes and lizards were unclean. Moses felt like sacrificing one of the boys, or even both of them. But an experience Father Abraham had had with his son had taught his people that they were not to sacrifice their children. Then he had a sudden rush of genius to the head. Maybe 'I AM' would be satisfied with a bit of a child? The Midianites did not cut off the foreskin until the bridegroom's wedding night. Moses had been so glad he had been done already. But Zippy had not had the boys done. That was it! He was sure I AM would like to have a bloody foreskin. He grabbed his flint knife (for the desert peoples were still in the Stone Age, unlike the Egyptians), pressed it into Zippy's hand and told her to get to work on one of the boys. It was her duty as a wife to obey his every word, besides if she wanted her husband to survive the night, she had better get on with it. Zippy seized a surprised, half sleeping, Gershom, pushed him outside the tent, lifted up his ephod and swiftly performed the deed. But she could not restrain her anger. Stepping back into the tent, she flung the holy offering in the direction of – well let's say the lower part of Moses' torso, screeching "You bloody Hebrew half-caste! Why did I have to marry YOU!" or words to that effect. But Moses, still in agony, gratefully took the holy sacrifice, went outside and threw it on the little fire that guarded the tent against beasts of prey. There was soon a crackling sound and a pleasant aroma of cooking flesh. Imagining the pleasure that all this caused God, he crawled towards the bushes and there provided the struggling vegetation with a generous amount of fertilizer. In the morning Moses was in a cheery mood and ready to face a dozen pharaohs. The same could not be said of Zippy, nor of their son Gershom.

MEN FEAR WOMEN

'Moses feared God even more than he feared women.'

Could that be because there was no knowing whether someone whose name was 'I AM WHAT I AM' was male or female?

Most men are afraid of women; most husbands are afraid of their wives; they are also afraid of what is perceived as feminine, including the feminine in themselves. Patriarchy, male controlled religion, verbal misogyny, violence against women and pornography are all responses to this fear. Women naturally have great power over men because men need women sexually and women have the ability to make them feel small and failures. This is tragic because women, like God, desire to be loved and to be loved above all without fear.

Gays are feared by other men because gays do not fear women as 'straight' men do, and because gays highlight the feminine in men. Women are more at ease in the company of gay men because there is no fear on either side, no desperate need, and they may be loved for their own sake. Lesbians, however, are doubly feared because they are more emotionally independent of men than other women, and on that account have a fascination for some men expressed in their interest in lesbian pornography. The fascination of drag shows represents another twist to this fear.

The movements towards equality and to the acceptance by all of elements both masculine and feminine, far from being something to fear as some men hold, especially in the Christian Church and Islam, is to be welcomed because it relaxes the tensions all round and brings with it the possibility for all to be more at ease with themselves and their relationships.

MICHELLE
1 SAMUEL 19:11-18; 2 SAMUEL 12-19

History is written by the winners. David was a winner. His first wife Michelle was not. Princess Michelle, daughter of King Saul, fell in love with David, the good looking young buck at the royal court. (Her brother Jonathan was equally smitten.) David never said no to a good offer. Saul had thought to set David up with Michelle's older sister. But then he hit on the idea of using the budding romance between Michelle and David to rid himself of his young rival for the nation's popular acclaim. David could have Michelle if he could produce a dowry of 100 Philistine foreskins. David did better than this and produced 200 such foreskins. So David and Michelle got married. But Saul was still after David's guts. When Saul's soldiers surrounded the couple's home, Michelle saved David's life by helping him to escape through the window and dressing up a statue to make it look like David ill in bed.

David was now a fugitive. But Michelle still loved him and waited for him. The years passed. Then she heard that he had taken other wives who, unlike Michelle, had born David some children. David had moved on. Meanwhile, Saul married Michelle to a man named Palti who seems to have loved her. Perhaps the only genuine love she ever received. But as David' star rose after Saul and Jonathan had been killed in battle, Michelle again found herself a pawn in the power-struggle, and David got Michelle back. The poor woman was passed like a parcel from one man to another without any choice in the matter. Can we not imagine that she felt used?

David's antics on Ark of the Covenant Day were the last straw. His giving of himself visually to God, leaving nothing to the imagination was one thing; giving himself thus to all the women of Jerusalem, irrespective of class or status, was more than Michelle could take. She flipped her lid and spoke disrespectfully to the king. That was the end. She might be Saul's daughter, but HE was king now.

We remember David. Michelangelo makes a statue. We sing about him in our hymns – 'David's harp with solemn sound' , and Jesus is David's son, born in David's royal city. Michelle on the other hand is a blue-stocking, a prude, who failed to keep up with the new freedoms of the times. Or if you prefer, she was unspiritual, not appreciating the purely holy and pious intentions of God's anointed. Either way, Michelle is in the dustbin of history. She is a loser.

GOMER

(HOSEA, CHAPS 1-3)

Gomer was a prostitute, as was her mother and grandmother before her. She was well trained in the trade, the techniques and the pitfalls. She was lounging one day against the wall of the well, her pick up point at mid-day, a time when respectable women do not come to fetch water. Here comes an unusual visitor. She knew who he was – everybody did, but she had never seen him come this way at this time before. He was Hosea, the local prophet, and he came with a message. Yahweh, the God of Israel had told him to marry a prostitute. And here he was. Since she was the only prostitute on duty at the time, it was to him an obvious sign from God that she was the one. She was so taken aback that she found it difficult to think straight. The proposition seemed a good one. She would forsake her life of shame and uncertainty. She would have a good home, no shortage of food, and a respectable status in society. Hosea did a good trade in giving advice for a fee, and offered as a speciality blessings and curses, though he preferred blessings. Gomer decided to give it a try. They lived together reasonably happily for about three or four years, and had three children in quick session, which Hosea insisted on calling peculiar names. But she could put up with that. Her husband could not have been more attentive and kind. He never overworked her, indeed he did much of the housework himself, even some of the cooking. And he never looked at another woman. But Gomer was restless. She missed the companionship of her former sister prostitutes, and also the customers, many of whom were interesting and engaging characters, and often sought her company just for a chat. One day Hosea came home from reciting his prophesies in the market place to find that Gomer had gone. She had been seen hitching a lift in a wagon making its way north to Syria. There she sought work at her old job, but found it difficult since she lacked the connections she had had at home. Eventually she had to make use of a pimp, who virtually took over her life, as well as using her himself for a while as his sex partner. She now had the worst of both worlds and started to play up and give her manager a hard time. She had always been lively and sure of herself and now she organized her fellow prostitutes, male and female, to demand shorter working hours and a bigger share of the profits. But she was playing a dangerous game. The Manager bound Gomer hand and feet together with a couple of the other chief agitators, put them in an ox cart and drove them down south to Israel to the market place in Samaria and put them up for slaves. They were put on display as was the custom, stark naked. Someone told Hosea about this, or God spoke directly to him, and he went to the market, made the highest bid for her and set her free. Or rather he took her home and kept her closely confined.

What were Gomer's feelings when she stood there on a platform without a stitch on, for all to see? Did she bow her head in shame? Not likely!. Here was a proud woman, with a sense of independence and a thirst for freedom for herself and for womankind. She was used to being naked and to displaying her nakedness to effect. That caused her no problems. Perhaps she even thought, "If the great King David was unashamed to go naked in public, why should I be ashamed?" She was not ashamed of her profession either. It calmed a lot of men who otherwise would be out of control, and worried and wounded found solace in a friendly ear. Added to which, it seems Hosea got some good sermons out of his experience with her. She was actually instrumental in teaching him about God's eternal love and forgiveness. Will she run off again? Not impossible. She is a free spirit. Perhaps next time she will come back of her own accord.

LISA AND MARY

LUKE 1: 24-56

'Lisa got pregnant and stayed at home. In those days, people who couldn't have children had to put up with a lot of painful gossip. So Lisa said, "God's been good to me. I don't have to be ashamed any more!" (GOOD AS NEW)

It's significant that Luke, an enthusiast for the women's cause, opens his story of the 'Good News' of Jesus, not with the birth of Jesus himself, but with Mary, his mother, and her cousin Lisa. It is with them that the Christmas story begins. They are part of the Good News, the Good News for everybody and not just for some.

Lisa and Mary were separated by age. Lisa was probably about forty and Mary probably somewhere in her teens. They lived at opposite ends of the country. Mary lived in the north, in Nazareth, a place with a bad reputation. Lisa lived in the south, near to Jerusalem and Bethlehem. She was a priest's wife and presumably no stranger to high society. Yet these two women instinctively moved together and helped one another as friends at a crucial time for both their lives. They had a lot in common.

Firstly, they both knew what it was to be stigmatized. Lisa had failed to produce a child for Kerry, her husband. In their society infertility was assumed to be the woman's fault and was understood by the religious to be a sign of God's disapproval. Perhaps nothing was said to Lisa's face, but she would have been aware of a certain coldness and of wagging tongues behind her back. As for Mary, she was pregnant, as the other women of her little town were quite capable of picking up. She was not yet married and the identity of the father was a matter of speculation and gossip. She would soon be an unmarried mother unless some man did the decent thing. Mary's visit to her cousin, a long way away in those days, doubtless had something to do with avoiding awkward questions or glances when she went to fetch water from the well. The man who would find his closest friends and allies among the outcasts and marginalized, was himself outcast and marginalized from the word 'go'. This was something he shared with his mother Mary and his aunty Lisa before him. This family knew all about being stigmatized.

But despite being stigmatized, and despite all the attempts there might have been by the religious of the day to stamp Lisa and Mary as having been rejected by God, both believed the very opposite was the case. They each had a strong conviction, based on their own very personal experiences, that God had a particular love for them and that they had a special part to play in God's plans for the world. They must have been a great encouragement to one another. Mary spent three months in Lisa's company during the period of their joint pregnancy. They had much to talk about. Much of it would have been about babies and about their hopes for the future. The first-born was regarded by the Jewish people as specially dedicated to God. Every Jewish mother's greatest hope was that her son would turn out to be God's chosen leader, the Messiah, or at the very least, a prophet. Lisa and Mary had firm grounds for believing that in their cases their hopes would come true. I'm sure that if we had a chance to ask them, they both would tell us that during this exciting but difficult period, with its fears as well as its hopes, they could not have coped without the other.

Marginalized people stick together. That's why in the Gospels 'traitors and prostitutes' are often linked together as the chosen company of Jesus. Jesus joined them.. When Archbishop Tutu was asked why he was so enthusiastic about Gay Rights he replied, 'Freedom is not divisible. You cannot be in favour of freedom in your own cause and then deny freedom to others in their cause.' Despite all attempts to make Lisa and Mary feel 'out-of-it', they felt very much 'with-it'. So together they praise God. Mary it seems had a good voice, for she sang to Lisa a variation of a hymn they both knew well, the Song of Hannah. Although we think of it as Mary's song, it was sung by Mary with Lisa in mind. Hannah, like Lisa, had known what it was like to be childless. The song we know as 'The Magnificat' has become a regular hymn of praise in some churches, but often in a very proper and formal setting. It was a song of revolt, in which the weak and rejected, including women, are especially honoured by God, whereas the machos and bullies of society are left out in the cold. It should be the prime task of Christians in every age to seek out the victims, whatever they have been victimized for, and to welcome them into the very centre of their community and life. This rarely happens, but it does sometimes, here and there. Then the presence of Jesus is assured.

CHAPTER TEN

MEN TREATED BADLY

SAMSON
JUDGES CHAPS. 13-16

'Then Delilah said to Samson, "How can you say, 'I love you', when your heart is not with me? You have mocked me three times now and have not told me what makes your strength so great." Finally after she had nagged him with her words day after day, and pestered him, he was tired to death. So he told her his whole secret, and said to her, "A razor has never come upon my head; for I have been a Nazarite to God from my mother's womb. If my head were shaved, then my strength would leave me; I would become wek, and be like anyone else." (Judges 16: 15-17.)

Samson is portrayed in the Book of Judges as one of the judges. The word Judge is a bad translation. It means in the context of the book a charismatic leader. Samuel's birth was a bit iffy. A wandering sort of monk, a Nazarite, teetotal and vegetarian, told the wife of one Manoah that she was to have a baby. And maybe he ensured that she did, which was one of the tasks of a holy man in those days (See also Samuel). He requested that the offspring be also Nazarite and wear his hair hippy style, uncut. Samson was duly born and became a leader, inspired by the Spirit. But his abilities had more to do with his strong physique than his mental prowess. In Wales we would call him 'twp', (no English equivalent.) When he is said to have slain considerable numbers of Israel's enemies, it was probably at the head of an expeditionary force, though undoubtedly his enthusiasm was an inspiration. When he is described as having killed a lion single handed, we are judiciously told that it was young lion, probably not much more than a cub. But that is not how the 'weak up top' Samson saw it. Maybe he was an early Israelite version of Don Quixote. No sooner than his sexual feelings started to have their influence on him he fell in love with a Philistine. (A pre-cursor of the Palestinians) That was not a sensible thing to do. So we are all set for Shakespeare and Romeo and Juliet. Here is love accross the unbridgeable boundaries of irreconcible races. Well done Samson for trying. Well done for discounting race in making a choice. Unfortunately this woman did not prove trustworthy and so Samson made a present of her to his male friend! Strong Samson may have been, but not very good at judging character, nor at personal relationships in general. Eventually he got involved with another Philistine woman, Delilah, who was a right man-slayer. O dear, will he never learn? Afraid not! Somewhere along the line someone had told him that his strength was in his hair. One of his companions taking advantage of his simplicity and pulling his leg maybe? But it got stuck in his mind and he believed it totally and implicitly. Fatal as it would prove. Hairiness is often associated with manliness, though a wider knowledge of life will teach you how unreliable is hair as a guide. Samson did not have that knowledge, nor was he up to obtaining it. He thought that if he ceased to be hairy he would become effeminiate, weak like a woman. And his weak mind ruled his body. Weak minded or no, Samson comes over as a loyal and likeable chap who deserved better treatment. He trusted in God after his own lights, and according to those lights he was at last vindicated. A hero in his own way.

NABOTH
1 KINGS CHAPTER 21.

'..there occured an incident involving Naboth, who had a vineyard in Jezreel adjoining the palace of King Ahab...'

Here is Naboth, a man whose misfortune was to have a property next to the King of Israel. We know his name, which is a wonder. He stands for many whose names are unknown, mowed down by the State. Ahab is the King, with the trappings of monarchy, in a position to get whatever he wants, or so his nasty wife Jezebel tells him. But he has the mind of a baby with his toys. Obsessed and frustrated he has the power to break one that momentarily annoys him. But he is not powerful at all, but weak, and dependant like all humans on circumstance, a prisoner. So Gloriana, Elizabeth I, the greatest and most successful of English monarchs, the object of thirteen assassination attempts. She was lonely without a true loving companion apart from her old nurse and fellow Welsh woman, Blanche Parry, who holds her in her arms and calms her fears in bed at night. Or one might think of Louis XIV of France imprisoned in his beautiful big toyhouse Versailles, 'The Sun

King' the despot of despots expecting during his long reign to be assassinated any moment, and fighting continual wars vainly trying to extend his territory, leaving a people, impoverished, resentful and ripe for revolt. On the other side from Ahab is Elijah, the prophet, representing the religious who too little and too late protest against the blatant injustices of society. He stands up for God and righteousness, but doesn't save Naboth. Piggy in the middle is Naboth who represents the individual. Wooed by the State to enrich his lands and gain favour with the current idiot on the throne in exchange for being the person he is. He stands firm and loses his life. Just like the hundreds and thousands of gay people who are driven to misery, illness and suicide, just because those with power don't like them, and because the churches cannot get their act together on sexuality in time to save them. And there are many others who die simply for being who they are. The soldiers who are shot because they will not go on killing others, and those who are killed or maimed anyway. The glorious and inglorious dead we celebrate every Armitice Sunday in religious services. Names are named, but most are forgotten, like Naboth. Forgotten, but not quite. Every one written on the hands of God, they hold their candles alight.

JEREMIAH

'Do not say, "I'm only a child," for you must go to all to whom I send you and say whatever I command you. Do not be afraid of confronting them, for I am with you to rescue you, the God whose name is 'I AM' declares.'

Then God stretched out a hand and touched my mouth, and said to me:

'There! I have put my words into your mouth.
Look, today I have set you
over the nations and kingdoms,
to uproot and the knock down,
to destroy and to overthrow,
to build and to plant.'

(Jeremiah 1: 4-10)

I studied for my 'A' levels at Bristol Cathedral School. There I was nicknamed 'Jeremiah'. It was not meant to be affectionate. For over a year I was bullied. I was a Baptist in an Anglican school, an alternative that was not tolerated by some. They may also have sensed that my manliness, according to their way of looking at things, seemed to be somewhat lacking. I didn't handle it very well. I can't say that I was very tolerant either. Like Jeremiah I had a sharp tongue. Like Jeremiah I was a pacifist, but that did not mean that I did not retaliate. I did not understand the language of my alien environment, and by the time I did I had irretrievably made a fool of myself. I know how Jeremiah felt, "I'm only a child. I do not know how to speak." Some Christians have a strong sense of call to champion some cause or make some protest, or provide some alternative to what is being generally offered in the contemporary world. And you do not have to be a Christian to be that way, of course. Such rebels include all those who have campaigned for LGBT liberation, whatever their religion or none. In particular in the Christian churches, the fortresses of predudice and authoritative ignorance, remain dauntingly tough. However we have joyed to see the 'kingdoms of this world' entrenched in Christian minds and hearts beginning to crumble and fall. God is on our side and we shall overcome. From the start Jeremiah was rebellious and questioning. He was to have many a battering and many a close shave. He was a member of the priesthood and the establishment. But he was on the wrong side of both. He was thrown into a disused well , left to sink in the mud and only just rescued by a black African. (Chapter 38) Yet he and God achieved things together on an international scale. Although he often felt that God was a hard taskmaster, we can see from our perspective the two of them getting on with a mammoth task together, winning through, and actually the best of mates.

You're Needed Men of God

You're needed, men of God;
So less of trivial things;
Spend time on care and mindfulness;
It's Love the New World brings.

Men play a special part,
as do our sister mates;
Apply your muscles and your art;
A world in torment waits.

There is no ideal type;
No manly protocol;
No one excluded for their tastes;
No brother made a fool.

Pattern yourself on Him
who is the friend of all;
He wept and cried as well as toiled;
So champion those who fall.

They are not fully men
Who spurn their softer side;
If you engage your fullest self,
you set it to abide.

Have courage, men of God
Hold cross and grave in mind,
Good Friday pain and Easter light,
That way your role you'll find.

(John Henson. After 'Rise up, O men of God!'
W.P. Merrill 1867-1954)

CHAPTER ELEVEN

SONG OF SONGS 'GOD'S 'YES' TO SEXUALITY

(Song of Songs 1 John 4: 7-21 NRSV.)

I recall the remark of a panellist on T.V. in a discussion in the 1980s on the vexed issue of sexual education. She was against it in schools, and I rather think against it altogether. She had obviously been selected for the programme to represent 'traditional' values. She said, "They will only be interested in the dirty bits. A civilised country keeps its sewers underground." At about the same time, a leading policeman, responsible for fighting crime in Manchester, by the name of Anderton talked about people with A.I.D.S., "drowning in their own cess-pit."

The notion that sex=dirt is implicit in the attitude of many Christians and still lives on in a society which was guided by the Church in sexual matters throughout most of the history of the western world. A 'dirty joke' means a joke with a sexual content. The joke may well be dirty on other grounds. It may have an edge which demeans and degrades other people. But for many some sexual content is sufficient to class the joke as dirty. 'A dirty weekend' is a weekend in which it is thought that sexual activity, possibly illicit, but not necessarily so, has taken place. A man may talk about a dirty weekend with his wife.

This equation of sex with dirt is the popular spin-off of the Gnostic heresy. The Gnostic heresy most obviously identified as such in the first few centuries of the Church's history, is based on the idea that body and spirit are in competition. The body is evil and the spirit is good. There is a fight between them to the death.

Paul, the leading thinker of first century Christianity seems to have been influenced by Gnosticism while at the same time trying to combat it. Though it may be argued that he uses Gnostic language in a totally un-Gnostic way. For Paul it is not body and mind that are opposites. Both body and mind may be either spiritual or of the flesh, depending on whether or not they are indwelt by Christ. Gnosticism seems to have entered the world from Persia where the dominant religion, Zoroastrianism, was based on the dualism of good and evil, a competition between light and darkness. This influence blended easily with the Jewish laws and customs relating to hygiene, which had begun by being soundly based on concern for health, but by the time of Jesus had become matters of ritual. This is true, for example, of the rules relating to circumcision. It became almost as important that this be performed on the eighth day as that it be performed at all.

There is no unified view on sex in scripture, nor on much else for that matter. But scripture does hold an alternative view to the sex=dirt view. In Genesis (1.17), sex is a essential part of what God made and 'saw that it was good'. Sex belongs to the creation in which God delights, and not just a necessary evil, as we have been programmed to think.

The Song of Songs is a piece of Jewish eroticism. It has, therefore, always been an embarrassment to Christians. How often, if ever, has any of us heard a reading in a service, a sermon or a discussion in a Bible study group of the Song of Songs? One of the most dishonest of the Church's attempts to shield the innocent 'believer' from the true nature and meaning of the scriptures, was its allegorising of the Song. People were told that it was a poem about Christ and his Church, Jesus being the bridegroom and the Church the bride. Even though the Church rarely goes so far as to try this one on nowadays, the language of the Song is still used in songs of piety relating to Jesus. He is the "Rose of Sharon and the Lily of the Valley." "I am his and he is mine" or "Blessed assurance *Jesus is mine*", and a more recent chorus of the very silly variety, "he brought me into the banqueting hall and his banner over me is love." I suppose it is just as well the singers don't realise the original meaning of these words. They would be frightfully embarrassed! (Or not, as the case may be.)

The Song is a series of poems containing various scenes of a sexual nature. Some think they may have been recited or sung at a Jewish wedding. Rather less comfortably from our own standpoint, they may have been intended as an accompaniment to an orgy. More likely they form an entertainment celebrating the joys of sex in music, dance and pageant. There is no mention of marriage, family or procreation. There are lovers. But, sorry, dear prudes, there is no bride or groom! The Song of Songs celebrates at high pitch the reality that women possess sexual feelings which are there for them to enjoy. Much indeed in the Song is written from the women's perspective, so that today we may posit the probability of a female author, or maybe a group of authors containing at least one female. The notion that women could or should enjoy sex was denied by the Church until recently. Only men (and perverted women) had a sex drive. The role of the woman in sex was to bite on an apple and think of England! (Or whatever your native land.)

The twentieth century saw a sexual revolution to match anything that came about in the way of change in the other great revolutions in the human story. The ideas of the enlightenment at last filtering through, Freudian psychology, new freedoms, social and individual, the liberation of women, science and medicine have all combined amazingly to make the Song of Songs one of the most important and relevant books in the Bible. How long before the Church notices? The attitude of the Church to the sexual revolution has been almost entirely negative. Its object has been to hold the line. It has not been very successful in line-holding, but it has caused a lot of tension and a lot of guilt. It has sought to confine sexual experience within marriage. It has sought to limit it there to a narrow range of activity – the Church has never been happy about manuals of sex which widen the repertoire. Such manuals are not 'wholesome'. The church has sought to prevent displays of nudity or the portrayal of sexual activity on stage or film, or its detailed description in literature. The Catholic Church has opposed contraception and education on family planning and has been joined by others in opposition to abortion on any grounds whatever, and continues to oppose divorce and re-marriage. The whole Church has continued to disapprove of relationships which lack the necessary license from church or state and by and large to deny the possibility of love between people of the same sex. The church has dragged its feet on issues of equality for women; has continued to cast the woman in a servile role, perpetuates forms of marriage service in which the woman is seen as a property passed from father to groom and so on. Overall, the Church continues to use guilt about sex as a means of exercising power over its declining constituency.

The impression many Christians give is that they would prefer it if sex did not exist; they would prefer not to talk about it, especially not in detail. Those who take a more liberal attitude are likely to be accused of undermining society, destroying the family, 'lowering standards', and so on.

What are the results of the Church's Attitude? Firstly, the Church displays its ignorance. Because we have turned our back on the sex revolution, there is an important amount of human life and experience we do not understand and cannot therefore comment intelligently upon. This includes many of the discoveries of psychological and sociological research. Christians are not interested in ideas or even in facts that do not tie in with their own preconceptions. The Church also remains ignorant of much of what has been learnt by experiments in relationships which have been carried on by ordinary people without the Church acting as Nanny. People have been discovering themselves in their own way. They have things to tell us, but WE only want to tell THEM.

The Church insults people by calling them sinners simply because they have a different pattern of sexual behaviour from what Christians regard as right and proper. We assume that because people have different moral guidelines from ours that they have no morals. That is an insult, because it is not the truth. The Church labels as lust any sexual behaviour which does not obey its rules, whereas people know when they are experiencing genuine love, care and commitment. Our spitting on their experience of love is an insult that disinclines them to listen to anything else we have to say sympathetically.

We have perpetuated the Gnostic heresy. We are incapable, because of our hang-ups, of appreciating the beauty of the human body, the pleasure of physical contact, the variety of sexual experience. I would say that the Church has been as responsible as any pornography for treating sex as something nasty and ugly. Indeed the Church has provided the repression upon which pornography feeds.

In all this the Church has failed to be light for the world. We have failed to give a positive message. We should have been teaching people how to love and to use the gift of sex as a tool for loving, instead of leaving it to secular agencies. We should have been supporting people and congratulating them and rejoicing with them whenever love emerges, instead of joining with 'Disgusted of Tonbridge Wells.' (The famous frequent writer at one time to BBC Radio of letters protesting about something or other on their programmes. His letters invariably began "I was disgusted last night to hear....etc.) Counsellors encounter a steady stream of people who have been scarred by their experience at the hands of other Christians who have judged them and ostracized them for their personal behaviour. The Church has made such a mess of sex that it would not be unfitting for it to deny itself the privilege of making authoritative pronouncements on anything relating to the subject for the next fifty years, and instead to start listening and learning. We have a lot of catching up to do. It would help to re-instate the Song of Songs into the canon of scripture and to listen to what it has to say to us.

CHAPTER TWELVE

THE MOTHERS OF JESUS

Matthew's Gospel begins with a list of the ancestors of Jesus. The purpose is plain. This gospel was compiled in the main to convince Jewish readers of the claims of Christianity. It was thus important to establish that Jesus was of the correct descent to qualify him to be Messiah. He must be of genuine Jewish stock, descended from Abraham and Jacob, and more especially he must be descended from David, the great king and Messiah-prototype. Then it had to be demonstrated that Jesus was born the first-born to his parents, thus dedicated to God, and in Bethlehem. Perhaps Matthew did not care what sort of ancestors Jesus had providing these provisions were satisfied. However, we are used to the idea that a person's character and culture are largely dependent on our parents and grandparents at the very least, and the Jews had an even stronger understanding of this link. With a very weak concept of an after-life, the ancient Israelites looked to their children as the hope of the continuation of their life in the future. A son was more than a physical product of his father. He was his father reproduced, repeated and continued. That is why disobedience to parents was regarded as such a great sin, punishable by death. Disobedience meant that the natural identity of character and will between father and son had been broken. So we must expect something of Jesus to be perceived in his ancestors and it would be interesting from that point of view to study the whole list carefully. Here we look at five of them, the women.

Matthew's mention of female ancestors of Jesus is surprising. The climate of Jewish religion at this time was heavily patriarchal, women little more than chattels, excluded from full worship by dint of ritual impurity connected with their monthly periods. Luke, the Gentile writer, is generally regarded as the champion of women. But when he sets forth his genealogy he only mentions the male ancestors of Jesus. So Matthew is obviously determined to make a point. Jesus is a complete human being who inherits female as well as male characteristics. Matthew chooses to mention five women only. Five is the symbolic number often used to denote the people of Israel, bound together by the five books of the law. It also means that Matthew has to make a selection. There are important women, well-known names to the devout of Israel, Matthew does not mention, in particular Sarah, Rebecca and Leah, the mothers of the race. The five he chooses to mention are highly significant and quite startling in view of what was known about them. They are TAMAR, RAHAB, RUTH, BATHSHEBA, styled as 'the wife of Uriah', and MARY. Matthew seems to be saying that women, excluded from full recognition and status in the old Israel, become the very symbol of the new Israel.

We are going to look in some detail at the experiences of the women mentioned in Matthew's list. They are all Old Testament figures, including Mary, as will be explained. But inasmuch as they are true and fitting ancestors of Messiah, they prefigure the New Testament, the New Covenant of liberation introduced by Jesus. We shall see how they promote the woman's cause. We shall also think about the men with whom they were associated and see how they too were enlarged and liberated by their women.

TAMAR

(GENESIS 38)

The story of Tamar forms part of the family history of the Israelite tribes. Judah, one of Jacob's twelve sons, has married a Canaanite woman, Shua. Tamar whom he selects to be the bride of his eldest son Er is also probably a Canaanite, for her name is linked with the Canaanite goddess Ishtar. Her husband dies – the assumption was that God had punished him for some sin, the usual explanation at that time for untimely death. According to the custom it was now the responsibility of Judah's second son Onan to take her as his wife and provide children who would be understood as carrying on the line of his late brother. Onan, instead of fulfilling this duty, when he had intercourse with his wife failed to send his semen into her womb, and this was given as the explanation of his early death. Judah's third son, Shelah is at this time too young to take responsibility for Tamar, so she has to go back to her father's home until he grows up. Tamar now works out a strategy to get herself a child to see that she is properly looked after. She disguises herself as a prostitute, propositions her father-in-law Judah, and when later she is discovered to be pregnant, thereby meriting the death penalty for adultery, she reveals the name of the father. Judah acknowledges he has treated Tamar badly. She gives birth to twins, and one of these, Perez, becomes the main heir and the ancestor of Jesus.

This is the story of a woman who gets the better of men in a man's world by ingenuity and courage. At the beginning of the story we have the common scenario in which a woman is blamed for everything. By implication Judah blames Tamar for the deaths of his first two sons for he is afraid that if she marries his third son the same will happen to him. (v11) Tamar would also according to the thinking of the time be implicated in Onan's inability to have full intercourse with her – she was failing to please her husband in some way. The narrator of the story in a revolutionary way puts the blame firmly on the men. It is Onan who fails his wife. It is Judah who has failed to provide properly for his daughter-in-law. (v.26) It is Judah who has obliged Tamar to adopt extreme measures, involving her further humiliation in the role of the prostitute. Men must take the blame for prostitution! It is interesting that William Barclay, a well-known Scottish commentator of the 1950s still put the blame on Tamar calling her a 'seducer and adulteress'. He had not read the story very carefully!

In the male society portrayed in the story, the woman's needs are totally ignored. Tamar exists simply to provide heirs in the patriarchal line. Again, the narrator helps us to see things from the woman's point of view. She needs a man to give her protection and status. There was no other option at that time. But she also needs the affection of an appreciative partner, and she desires a child, for her own sake, not just for the man's.

The story touches on some very sensitive themes.

(1) **Masturbation.** Traditionally Onan's behaviour has been used to denote masturbation as a sin. This is a misuse of the

text. Onan was not masturbating in the generally accepted sense of the word – he was not having sex on his own. He was using someone else to gratify his lusts in a selfish way, without consideration for the other's feelings. The Onan story raises questions about mutual masturbation in the sense of sex that is divorced from care. This may occur inside or outside marriage. It is the lack of mutual care and sensitivity in sex that should be regarded as inappropriate. Solo masturbation can be regarded as positive good if it protects the object of lust from abuse. Mutual masturbation with agreement and understanding may also be a reasonable way of avoiding unwanted pregnancy, or of protecting a partner from a degree of intimacy not wanted at that stage.

What should our feeling towards Onan be? He is trapped by a social system that ignored the feelings of individuals in just the same way as Tamar was trapped. He was obliged to try to have sex with someone for whom he had no natural feelings. He may also have had a common male problem, that of premature ejaculation. What we see portrayed is a system which was intended to provide for the needs of society, but which fell far short. It is a warning against any system imposed by Church or society. It applies to the institution of marriage when those who are not suited or ready for marriage come under pressure to be married, or when there is pressure to remain in marriage on those who are desperately unhappy.

2) Prostitution. At the time of the story prostitution had an honoured place in society. Prostitutes were frequently attached to temples and associated with worship, in particular with fertility rites. Prostitutes made money for the temple and provided males with a sexual outlet to prevent anti-social behaviour. Verse 21 suggests Judah mistook Tamar for a temple prostitute, believing he was performing a religious function.

He had also lost his wife and was lonely. He had fulfilled the customary period of mourning which had included abstention from sex. So the narrator probably does not wish to imply Judah is doing anything wrong in seeking a prostitute. However, the point comes across that in some social situations a woman's plight can be so desperate that prostitution is her only recourse. Judah is to blame, and the male sex, for putting Tamar in this position. Despite her courage and ingenuity, what she is obliged to do is degrading.

So we have a sympathetic view of prostitution from the woman's point of view – Tamar is not blamed for taking this extreme measure; and from the man's point of view – he is lonely and missing his wife. The blame lies with social convention. There ought to have been social provisions that would have made Tamar's degrading stratagem unnecessary.

3) Incest. This is probably not a major theme in the story. Adultery is regarded as the sin that merits death, because it has to do with the violation of property. (See Deut 22: 23-24) Even though no one wants Tamar, she is still regarded as family property. If anything, incest is dealt with by the narrator favourably, inasmuch as the result is to secure Judah's lineage, the prime consideration in patriarchal society. (For a damning treatment of incest we must turn to the story of another Tamar, the sister of Absolom, David's son – 2 Samuel.13)

What effect did all this have on Judah? He was not horrified by the thought that he had committed incest, but rather about the way he had treated Tamar previously. A revolution has taken place in his mind and character. He could still at this point have shielded himself behind the social system he was part of. Tamar had deceived him. She had tricked him and brought disgrace on him. He could have stuck to the rules and had her executed. But Tamar succeeds in awakening something we can identify as 'conscience'. There is the morality of rules and social custom. But the only morality that counts in God's eyes is the way we treat one another, rules or no rules. There is no rule that can deal with kindness or unkindness. But we all know the difference, and we all know which is right and which is wrong. That is why this story prefigures Jesus who stressed the principle 'I will have mercy and not sacrifice.' Gentle treatment of one another is preferable in God's eyes to religious observance or codes of ethics. We do not know the end of the story, whether the household of Judah became a happier home as a result of Tamar's stand. We would like to think so. As the mother of the heir she would have an honoured position. Judah does not take her for his wife. But it would be nice to think that their close physical and emotional encounters brought a greater sensitivity and understanding between them as people.

The incredible thing is the singling out by Matthew of Tamar as an ancestor of Jesus. Matthew is telling us that the birth of Jesus resulted from a previous incestuous relationship, and moreover, one of the parties played the prostitute. This does not mean that Matthew is extolling or condoning incest. What he is saying is that someone born of such a relationship should not have any stigma attached. Religion delights in inflicting stigmas on people. The 'bastard', 'the unmarried mother', 'the old maid', 'the pervert', the 'divorcee', the 'ex-convict'. Once the stigma has been put on it is made to stick, often for more than one generation. The message of this story is in line with the Christian 'Good News', that whatever has happened in the past does not count. Tamar's unconventional morality is not held against her, nor Judah's against him. The blessing (that is the stream of goodness and God's favour) is passed on from Tamar and her son Perez to Boaz and Ruth. It is the blessing given to them at their marriage. It is passed on to David and then to Jesus who is of the tribe of Judah, the tribe that preserved these family stories with pride. A truly Christ-like Church will not put stigmas on people, nor go easy on church members who stigmatise.

RAHAB

('GOOD-AS-NEW' BARBARA OR 'BABS'.)
(JOSHUA 2 AND 6:17-20)

Rahab is an Old testament character who is honoured among the people of the New Testament. Not only does Matthew give her a place as an ancestor of Jesus, but the writer of Hebrews (likely Priscilla) puts Rahab in a prominent position in her roll-call of faith (11:31). She also has honourable mention from James, the brother of Jesus in his letter. (2:25) This suggests that Rahab was a revered ancestor in the family of Jesus.

Babs assisted the Israelites in the conquest of Jericho. She was a Canaanite and a prostitute. When Joshua sent spies into Jericho they made for the local brothel. They were combining business with pleasure. A visit to the prostitute was very good cover. Prostitutes catered for all sorts and they would be often visited by strangers from outside the town. They knew a lot, but had a code of honour to protect their customers. If a prostitute betrayed her customers it would be likely to damage her trade. The story is straightforward. In return for sheltering the spies, protecting them from the town police, and helping them to escape, Babs and her family were spared when Jericho was captured and everyone else slaughtered.

From the Israelite point of view Babs was a courageous woman who opted for the true God and for the future. But from an independent point of view she was a traitor who betrayed her country's secrets to the enemy. Her principle motive was her own survival. It is a classic case of moral or immoral depending on whose side you are on. The fact that she is a prostitute receives no condemnation in the story. Her profession also exonerates her from the judgement 'traitor' to a certain extent, for she serves the human race and is above loyalty to tribe, class and religion. Prostitute, traitor, foreigner – her blood mixes with that of the chosen race and she becomes the mother of Boaz and thus great, great grandmother of David. She could very easily been forgotten.

Most scholars agree that it is unlikely that Matthew, the disciple of Jesus, wrote the gospel with his name. But Matthew does appear in the gospel as a tax-collector who becomes a follower of Jesus and invites Jesus to a party. Tax collectors were quislings. They served the Romans. They were hated by their own people, especially by the Pharisees who called them 'sinners', linking them with prostitutes who were probably the only people who would keep them company. The gospel writer sees Babs as a precursor of the New Covenant which included prostitutes and traitors amongst its members. It is a reminder to the Church that the religion of Jesus gave no halo of respectability to the well-behaved, but reached out to embrace those who had no claims to respectability and were rejected by the society of their day.

RUTH

The book of Ruth was probably a piece of post-exilic propaganda. When the Jews returned from Babylon many of them had married foreign wives. A strict party emerged under Nehemiah and Ezra that preached racial purity. The writer of Ruth writes from the opposite point of view. But the book is not just about racial tolerance. The returning exiles are symbolized in the book by two women returning from the foreign land of

Moab in a earlier period of Israel's history, one of them herself a foreigner. Amazingly the author chooses women to represent the new restored Israel returning from exile. Does this mean that women had been more loyal to their faith in exile than the men, in much the same way as the women in the gospels were more loyal to Jesus at the time of the cross? The book of Ruth must have been written by a woman. Everything is seen and described so clearly from the woman's point of view and there are even examples of the language of positive discrimination. (e.g. Naomi urges Ruth to return to her 'Mother's House 1.8 whereas the normal expression was 'Father's House' as in the case of Tamar.)

Three women stand at the crossroads. They have lost their men. By means of accident and tragedy they have achieved independence. They can make their own decisions without reference to men. Naomi decides to return to her own country. Ruth ignores Naomi's advice and insists on returning with her. In doing so she makes vows to Naomi..

'Do not press me to leave you or to turn back from following you! Where you go, I will go; where you lodge, I will lodge; your people shall be my people, and your God my God. Where you die, I will die – there I will be buried. I solemnly declare before God that nothing but death will part me from you.' (1:6)

Notice the similarity between these words of Ruth to Naomi with traditional Christian marriage services! I have even heard them read in a service of regular marriage between a man and woman in a Roman Catholic Church in 2007 as the 'Old Testament Lesson'. There was no attempt to explain the context or even that the words were said by Ruth to Naomi, but the reader ended confidently with the bidding, "This is the Word of the Lord.")

Ruth flies in the face of the conventional wisdom of the day that every woman needs a man. Naomi is her chosen partner. Orpah also makes her own decision. She has as much right to do so as the others. Her decision to behave more conventionally must not be seen as some kind of treachery to the feminist cause. Feminists and all other -ists must beware of exchanging one tyranny for another. Orpah loves her mother-in-law and her love is as sincere and passionate as Ruth's. But she cannot deny her own personality or change it. She cannot become sexually ambivalent like Ruth to meet new circumstances.

Ruth is the heroine of the story. Like Abraham she takes the ultimate leap of faith, abandoning home, natural family, culture, religion and convention to obey the call of God which is coterminous with her own destiny. The narrator explains to us that this destiny is to become the great-grandmother of David. But Ruth's faith is all the greater in that she does not, like Abraham, have a glimpse of what God has in mind, nor as yet has she embraced the religion of the God who leads her forward.

Boaz is the hero. He is portrayed as the ideal male who treats women with respect and is free from prejudice. Their courtship is worth studying. Ruth takes the initiative to provide for herself and Naomi by picking up the left-overs from the cornfields. May be she has a job in mind? Or a husband? Or the role of a concubine- a one-to-one prostitute? Boaz is interested. He asks 'to whom does this woman belong?' The reply is that she does not belong to anyone. She is the companion of Naomi. In the first conversation between Ruth and Boaz, Ruth is deferential, but it is a studied deference. She has come out with the purpose of finding favour and she has found it. Things are going her way. But in Boaz she finds a treasure, a true compliment to herself. Boaz is aware that a poor foreign woman without protection is open to abuse. He is not the sort of person to commit that kind of exploitation, and he protects her from abuse by others. His way is to woo Ruth in the gentlest way, instructing his men to leave extra sheaves of corn for her and refreshments. (8,14,17)

That Boaz is a relative of Naomi is a piece of luck. Naomi could have sought the protection of her nearest male relative if she had wished, but had not done so. Naomi has been embittered by her experiences and her attitude to Boaz seems cynical. She thinks that Ruth would be safer in the company of other women than staying near Boaz's servants as he had suggested. (2:21-23) She then sees the advantage of a match between Boaz and Ruth and with the wisdom of age and experience instructs Ruth as to how to go about it. She must make sure Boaz has had plenty to eat and to drink! Then she must make herself attractive by washing and dressing up. Then she must make a sexual pass at Boaz. Ruth lies down with Boaz while he is asleep and fondles his sexual parts. But Naomi's experience does not prepare her for Boaz. She has told Ruth that Boaz 'will know what to do'. Naomi is wrong. Boaz does not know what to make of it. He is flattered that Ruth has set her sights at an older man. (3:10) Naomi represents the sort of woman who believes men are 'all the same.' Boaz is truly grateful for a woman's attentions and does not take anything for granted. Ruth gives the instructions and tells Boaz to put his cloak over her to claim her as next of kin. Boaz is anxious, as the sun comes up, that no one will catch them together (3:14). This suggests they have breached the rules of respectability. In all this Boaz is the 'modern man', respectful and careful with regard to the opposite sex, willing to allow the woman to take the initiative and share in the decision-making without seeing this as a threat to his masculinity. He is not the next of kin, so has to put things right with the man who is. He takes Ruth as his partner out of choice and not from obligation. For a man and woman to do their own courting like this out in the fields, and to make their own match in this way, was quite revolutionary. Marriages were arranged by families in those days. There is a fairy-tale ending. Ruth, Naomi and Boaz live together, united.

Ruth is an ancestor of Jesus. Like Jesus she moves within the social conventions of the day, at the same time demonstrating a remarkable personal freedom. The considerate treatment of one person by another is more important than any rule. The fulfilling of one's true personal destiny is part of what it means to follow the way of God. (See Matthew 16:26) The gentle treatment of Ruth by Boaz prefigures the way Jesus dealt with women.

BATHSHEBA
2 SAMUEL 11.

Of the five women selected by Matthew as the ancestors of Jesus, Bathsheba alone is not given her name. She is referred to as 'the wife of Uriah'. This may be because Matthew thinks the reputation of Bathsheba is so bad that the very mention of her name is a cause of shame. Or the reference to Uriah may be reminding his readers of her story in brief. She was not by right the wife of David. David stole her from Uriah.

The relationship between David and Bathsheba was a great scandal. Their sin was adultery. Adultery according to Hebrew thought, at least to the time of the kings and beyond, had nothing to do with having more than one sexual partner. Polygamy was practiced by those who could afford it. Concubines and prostitutes also had an accepted place. Adultery was stealing someone else's wife or concubine. It was a matter of possession. Bathsheba belonged to Uriah. David in taking Bathsheba from Uriah was being greedy, as Nathan the prophet made clear in his sermon-parable to David. (2 Sam 12: 1-7)

Who do we blame for this disgraceful set of events involving not only adultery, but murder?

David, who was idling at home instead of leading his troops in battle. He saw Bathsheba bathing from his rooftop. He should have gone downstairs or looked the other way. Instead he sent for Bathsheba. Because he was the king she may have thought it unwise to refuse him. David's attraction for Bathsheba was 'lust'. The murder of Uriah was a crime to cover a crime.

Bathsheba was bathing in a place where she must have known she could be seen by the king or his courtiers. She may have been bored with her life with Uriah and had ambitions to be a lady of the court. It would have taken courage to refuse the king. But she had the perfect excuse. She was still ritually impure after her monthly period.

Uriah does not seem to have been a very enthusiastic husband. When David urges him to visit his wife so that Bathsheba's pregnancy will be attributed to Uriah, he turns down the offer. He uses religion as an excuse. (vs 8-13.) Nobody comes out of this story very well.

Perhaps mostly to be blamed is a social/sexual system in which people, especially women, are thought of in terms of property. This means Bathsheba is locked up in purdah for as long as her husband is away from her. Her behaviour, bad though it is, may be seen as a move towards personal fulfilment. Ultimately, though not without intervening distress, her quest for personal fulfilment is successful. Her breaking of the irrational and repressive law with regard to monthly periods is also courageous. David too is in part the prisoner of a system of monarchy whereby all his subjects, Bathsheba and Uriah included, are regarded as his property. In any land other than Israel, Nathan would have been executed for his insolence. Only because David was a particularly godly man could his conscience be called to account by Nathan. Uriah also has a piece of property in his wife that he does not particularly want. He prefers to be with the boys. But he cannot do anything about it, except neglect her. The system was unfair. Men could have concubines, women could not. A social system in order to be true to the God of love and justice must create the environment in which people can care for one another and encourage one another to develop their personalities to the full. If marriage or bonded friendship is an agreement between two people to do this, then it is a godly and a gospel thing. If it is the possession of one person by another or mutual possession, then it is anti-gospel and in danger of ending in tragedy.

This is a messy story with little that is positive to teach us. It is the sequel that is remarkable. Because David repents and accepts God's rebuke, he is allowed to keep Bathsheba, and it is her son, Solomon, who follows David as king. The story underlines the fundamental Biblical theme of forgiveness. In the Hebrew scripture, when someone who has sinned repents, then God forgives and the system of punishment is reversed. The Christian scriptures go beyond this. Jesus prays, "Loving God, forgive them. They do not know what they are doing." God forgives even without repentance. Jesus' qualification for forgiveness is not repentance but the willingness to forgive others. "Forgive us the way we wound you, as we forgive others when they wound us." "If you do not forgive others their wrongs, neither will your heavenly parent forgive the wrong things you do."

The story of Bathsheba shows that God does not only forgive. God tops up forgiveness. God demonstrates that it is possible to redeem and reconstruct out of the worst human scenario. If Jesus had been born of a pure, sinless line, there would have been nothing for God to work on as a challenge. God chose to deal with the problems of men and women by entering into a flesh and blood relationship with them.It was very annoying to the Pharisees, as it probably would have been annoying to Nathan, a good and brave man, that Jesus, God's representative, chose as his special friends people like Bathsheba and David, not in the sense of their being regal, but in the sense of their being naughty. Jesus was not interested in someone's past history, only in their future progress.

MARY

Of all five female ancestors of Jesus, Mary is the one it is the most difficult to say anything about, because so much has been said about her already, most of it pure fantasy. Some have turned her into some kind of goddess to be worshipped together with her son, sometimes, it looks very like, in preference to her Son. Others have reacted to the worship of Mary by doing their best not to think about her at all. Fundamentalists and creedal Christians are prone to defend the virgin birth instead of being interested in Mary, just as they concentrate on defending a particular view of the atonement while having very little interest in Jesus. The references to Mary in the scriptures are few and tell us almost nothing about what sort of person she was. We know much more from scripture of the character of Ruth.

Many scholars think the birth narratives an invention. But even if we believe them to be based on fact, there is still not much to go on. Those references to Mary that occur apart from the birth stories are unpromising for those who want Mary to be an object of adoration or even of admiration.

For Matthew, Mary is the fifth in a series of female ancestors, each illustrating some form of sexual deviancy. Mary he portrays as an unmarried mother. This is the reality, whether or not you believe in the virgin birth. When Joseph accepted her as his future bride, she was well on the way to giving birth and to becoming the cause of a public scandal. Matthew does not, like Luke, tell us how a messenger from God visited Mary to calm her anxiety. Matthew concentrates on the kind feelings of Joseph and his honourable behaviour in saving Mary from shame. We are told nothing of Mary's feelings or behaviour at the time. She is given no character at all. The narrative does not state in certain terms that there is no human father, simply that the origin of the child is God's Spirit, as indeed is true for every living being. God's Spirit can operate as easily through a man's semen as through a woman's womb and usually operates through both. The word traditionally translated 'virgin', in the original Hebrew language of the quotation from Isaiah means simply 'young woman' or young woman who has not previously had a child. The idea of a virgin birth probably originated from a distaste for the sexual act, a distaste that entered Christianity via the Gnostic heresy.

Other religions also had stories of virgin births. Christians had to keep up! The friends and neighbours of Mary and Joseph would have been amused by such an idea. As it was, they would have enjoyed a good gossip. Some would have admired Joseph for his kindness; others would have felt sorry for him; others would have held him in contempt for not insisting on his rights –he should have brought Mary to court. For Mary there would have been little sympathy at all. She had been a bad girl! Even if Joseph was the father, Mary would still get the blame. It would be regarded as beyond argument that Mary had seduced her boyfriend and defiled him. That was the way society thought in those days, and that is the way some judges in rape cases still think today. Christian piety has sought to rescue Mary from the wagging tongues. The tongues continued to wag into the adulthood of Jesus. One rumour was that his father was a Samaritan. (John 8:48) Mary's plight brought out the best in Joseph, as it might have brought out the worst in another man. He is a true descendent of Boaz, sensitive and caring, and imaginative enough to see things from the woman's point of view.

Matthew puts Mary in the same company as incestuous Tamar, Rahab the prostitute, Ruth who loved another woman and played with a man in the cornfields, and Bathsheba the adulteress. He does so in order to say "These are the mothers of Emmanuel – GOD WITH US." (1:23) God's holiness and righteousness are not to be equated with respectability or sexual purity. God is interested in becoming a real human being with sex and by means of sex, regular or irregular. Matthew could so easily have done what Luke did and said nothing about the female ancestors of Jesus, or he might have mentioned some of the more respectable ones instead. The most obvious thing that draws these characters together is their lack of respectability and suitability to be the ancestors of God's Chosen. Matthew's Gospel is for the Jews, for people who are looking for a Jewish Messiah. But the author is as interested as the other gospel writers and Paul in challenging the Jewish pride of race. Tamar, Barbara and Ruth are ancestors of David as well as Jesus, and they are Gentiles. Bathsheba's first husband was also Gentile, a Hittite. Matthew, far from trying to establish a racial purity for Jesus says, "Yes, Jesus was of mixed origins. There were strong strains of Gentile blood. Jesus is not just the saviour of one People, he is the Saviour of the world.

The Gospel of Matthew more than the other gospels quotes the words of Jesus that challenge the hypocritical respectability of the Pharisees, especially in chapter 23. And in chapter 21:31 Jesus says, "Truly I tell you, the tax collectors and the prostitutes are going into the kingdom of God ahead of you."

And when the Pharisees are shocked at the way Jesus went to a party attended by social outcasts, Jesus said, "Those who are well have no need of a doctor, but only those who are sick. Go and learn what this means, 'I desire mercy, not sacrifice'. ' For I have not come to call the righteous but sinners." (9:13) In choosing his list of female ancestors, Matthew associates Jesus with 'sinners' in his origins as well as in his lifestyle. The word 'sinner' (that is, 'social outcast') is a word the Pharisees used to mark off certain categories of people from themselves. Jesus does not use the word except in reply to the Pharisees, indeed he does not even think in those terms. The mistake of the Pharisees is that they cannot see that the whole of humanity requires improvement, especially their own.

The humanity into which Jesus is born, of which he is a part and with which he unashamedly identifies himself, is a despised and victimized humanity. The story of Mary is told by the Church in such a way that brings in extenuating circumstances to save her from the charge of being an unmarried mother. But whether the story told that way is fact or fantasy does not really matter. There are no extenuating circumstances that can get round the involvement of all humanity in muddle and mess. Jesus did not try to avoid this involvement. Of his own choice he went in up to his neck and over his head in the muddy waters of the river Jordan. Whether Mary is an unmarried mother or not makes no difference at all to the extent of her involvement in the human predicament. She and Jesus are members of a family that has nothing to boast of on the grounds of moral righteousness. God does not begin to save humanity by being born in an oasis of purity called 'the immaculate conception'. God begins with those he already loves and favours, the most human of the human, the physical and spiritual descendents of Barbara, the bearers of the blessing of Tamar and Perez, Boaz and Ruth, David and Uriah's wife.

God's messenger to Mary came one day,
He said, "My name is Gabriel, okay?"
"I have surprising news for you-
I've called to say
You're going to have a baby-
Hooray, hooray, hooray!"

Some will cry 'shame' and turn their backs on you,
But you will gather friends both kind and true.
His origin's a mystery, but just for now;
A child for everybody!
That's the why and how!

Then Mary lost her fears and she replied,
"Whatever God thinks best I'm on God's side.
I'll sing a song of liberty and face the day.
I'm going to have a baby-
Hooray, hooray, hooray!"

Then Joseph did the decent thing – stood by;
"I'm going to be a Dad, so there, don't cry!
We'll travel down to Bethlehem,
There'll be less fuss.
Though many will be hostile,
This means 'God with us!'

So in the street outside the Inn Love came,
God's joy and peace to us in human frame;
And we can join the curious few who came to say,
"He is our little wonder!
Hooray, hooray, hooray!"

(John Henson.
After Sabine Baring-Gould 1834-1924)

CHAPTER THIRTEEN

THE CASTRATED MAN

(I am indebted to my dear and long-term friend Peterson Toscano for some of the insights of this chapter. In places I have copied his actual words)

'The sons which thou shalt beget
**They shall be taken away
and be eunuchs In the palace of the king of Babylon.**

Isaiah 39:7)

Howl ye, therefore…'
(William Walton
'Belshazzar's Feast' –
highly recommended listening.)

Today we have a great number of categories of sexuality. Human beings like to put people into boxes and tie the boxes up with sticky tape. That way they feel comfortable and assured that they know what is what, and how to cope with everybody, at least sexually. I think it was in my late teens that my mind was opened up to the fact that there were three, not two categories of sex – male and female, and something in between. This new category was medically described as 'homosexual', though subsequently found to have nothing to do with medicine. Later, towards the end of my university career the more user friendly word 'gay' appeared. In the late 1970s the 'Gay Christian Movement' also appeared and became a constituent part of 'ONE for Christian Renewal', of which I later became alternately Chairperson and Folder Editor. So all was well, and with the aid of a little education, which we would provide, the churches would gladly and joyfully celebrate an additional sex and its potential to increase the numbers of happy lovers. It did indeed take a little while before the churches, by and large, concluded that a new and a rampaging terror had entered the corridors of the Holy Place, and that measures should be taken forthwith to get rid of it. Some thought that compassion might be a better approach, until they found that gay people considered compassion patronizing. Others chose outright hate as their weapon – 'Love the Sinner and Hate the sin.' Surprising how this mindless slogan, not from the Bible by the way, is used almost exclusively against gay people, and never against religious pomposity and ignorance! Soon it became obvious that many hated the sinner more than they hated the sin, and many a vociferous Bible Basher was caught with his underpants down in a homosexual context. It seemed that what the ever righteous chiefly objected to was that these people were unashamed of their condition , instead of exploding in tears, like the Bible Basher before re-entering his pulpit to the applause of his doting mega-congregation.

Soon the Gay Christian Movement had problems of its own. Being gay was not so straightforward as gay people and their supporting buddies were inclined at first to assume. One shape did not fit all. First the women no longer wished to be called gay. "Please call us Lesbians. We are different from male gays." And so they are! (Some still prefer to continue to be called gay, however.) That was alright. We will be "The Lesbian and Gay Christian Movement" . Instead of GCM, get used to LGCM. But not for long! Because this was now the age of liberation, there was much bold experimentation, and wandering down alleys, and one thing that emerged was that many so-called 'straight' men, and women, appreciated a little something with their own sex from time to time, or even more often. The initial response of the leaders of LGCM was that this was unacceptable. People should get into their right boxes as quickly as possible and stay there. These people were promiscuous, fornicators, adulterers. Then surveys started to come out from the secular world , considered bone fide by psychologists and sociologists, that this ambivalent behaviour was practised at some time or another, to a greater or lesser degree, by a sizeable wedge of the population, and perhaps more. So now we had to think in terms of LGB and soon after LGBT because Transgendered and Transvestite people were now wishing to be heard, and about time too. In the early days they were forbidden attendance at our local GCM. "You have to draw the line somewhere!" Finally, (there is no finally), some people wanted the word 'Q' added, standing for 'Queer,' for those not belonging exclusively to any of the above categories, and who do not wish to be put into a box. Though perhaps by insisting on a box of their own they were doing so. But, please understand, they wished the freedom to be 'different'.

In the world of the Hebrew scriptures, there were also not two categories of sexuality but three. The third category was the eunuch. The eunuch was a non-productive male, usually castrated, and often castrated before puberty. This means they typically did not experience puberty. They missed the rush of testosterone bringing about the lowering of the voice, the development of body hair, facial hair, muscles, and over time, a prominent brow. They looked and sounded different from the men and women around them. The 'Castrati' continued as artificially created perpetual altos or even sopranos for the Cathedral choirs of the Roman Catholic Church until the eighteenth century, since only 'men' were allowed to lead in the sanctuary. Handel, who spent some time in Italy, composed some of his famous operatic roles for them. At the same time, as a Protestant, he disapproved of castration.

Eunuchs were highly prized in the world of the Middle East in ancient times. They were often highly intelligent men, taken captive by the Babylonians and Persians from the countries of their conquests, castrated, and then given prominent positions of trust in the government of the country, in the court, and as ambassadors. They could be trusted to rule the Harem because it was supposed they would constitute no threat to the women (perhaps a naive assumption), but more particularly they would be no threat to the ruling dynasty, since they would be incapable of producing heirs and forming a rival dynasty themselves. Later in the world of Islam, often the Grand Vizier in the court of the Sultan, second only in authority to the sultan himself, was a eunuch, for the same reason.

The situation was different among Jews. There is a law in the book of Deuteronomy (23:1) , which reads

'No man who has been castrated or whose penis has been cut off may be included among the Lord's people.'

This law could be later than the context of Moses and Mount Sinai in which it is set. It may reflect the horror of the exile in which so many of the younger nobility were taken into exile in Babylon and castrated. This also sometimes meant them compromising their religion and inherited customs in order to be loyal servants of the Babylonian and then Persian kings. The Hebrew view of life after death tended to be that a person's life was perpetuated in the life of their children. If they could physically produce no children, then their lives were 'cut off from the land of the living.' They had no future. From the time of the return from exile onwards there was a strong tendency to exclude from the Holy People, and the experience of their worship, anyone who for any reason whatsoever was considered to deviate from the norm. This exclusive aspect of Judaism may only have had much effect during periods when narrow religious bullies had sway. The situation may have been more relaxed at other times. Elijah does not seem to have been restricted by racism when he shared the home of a Syrian woman, nor by homophobia in his relationship with Obadiah. Jeremiah was rescued by a eunuch, a black Ethiopian, from a muddy pit he had been thrown into. It is unlikely he was either race prejudiced or prejudiced against eunuchs after that episode, and probably not before. (Jeremiah 38: 7-13) Daniel was parented and trained by a royal eunuch, Ashpenaz, and he may have been a eunuch himself.

We have seen the Book of Esther as an example of an early feminist winning her way to the top, and so it was. How can we have missed the fact that it could not have happened without the help of eunuchs? Without a word in the ear of the Persian king from the eunuchs Esther would have been far from court, an unknown orphaned Jewish young woman. Even in the palace she could not speak directly with her kinsman, Mordecai, who urged her to approach the king. She needed eunuchs to ferry messages to and fro, to set up the lunches for the king, and to instruct her in the sort of sex the king liked. Without them she would not have saved her people.

Being involved in a new translation of the scriptures obliged me to take a fresh look at the old stories. As I went along I got very excited by some of the new insights I made. The significance of the story of the conversion of the Ethiopian Eunuch is a good example. I was brought up to understand the story as an ideal text for an evangelical sermon. A missionary meets a non-Christian, tells him about Jesus and converts him. The story ends splendidly with an account of his baptism. Point of story – you need to be converted and baptised too!

What the preachers of my youth never said anything about as far as I can remember is what was very special about this particular case. This man was a eunuch – a castrated man. As I came to the part of the story where Philip the deacon and the castrated man read from the scroll of Isaiah together it suddenly hit me how appropriate the passage was to the case. The words are some of the most familiar from the Hebrew scriptures. In traditional translations they read: – 'he was led like a lamb to the slaughter.' The words are poetry and I tried to translate poetry into poetry. This is how it comes out in Good As New:-

> *He was driven like a lamb to the slaughterhouse-*
> *A sheep cannot argue with the shears.*
> *With nothing to say, put to shame in every way,*
> *There was no-one to calm his fears.*
> *His life was cut off; hope of children gone-*
> *Never was such injustice done.*

This is an extract from the anonymous prophet of Babylon whose writings can be found in the book of Isaiah, chapters 40 onwards. This particular extract looks very like a description of a man being castrated. We have always assumed that Philip related the passage about the sheep to Jesus. But the Greek says, 'Philip preached the good news about Jesus 'to him'. It suddenly struck me that what Philip was doing was relating the passage to the condition of the Ethiopian. Good As New I believe gets it right for the first time.

'Then Philip used this extract from the old book to explain to the castrated man how the good news of Jesus applied to HIM'

The eunuch in our story was an African, in charge of the treasure house of the Queen of Ethiopia. He was wealthy, high-placed, trusted with great responsibility. He was also a seeker after God. He used a holiday with pay to go on pilgrimage to Jerusalem where he had heard of an enlightened, dynamic religion. When he got there he went to see the temple and was looking forward to being shown around. What was he told? The rule was clear. "Sorry, our religion isn't for people like you." What could he do? He was excluded from the one true faith – permanently. He could not repent or have faith or promise to keep the law – he was snookered!

Was there anyone in Jerusalem who was embarrassed or felt regretful by the bitter disappointment of this man? There was someone. Someone gave him the scroll of Isaiah as a parting gift and said, "Have a read of that. I think you may find something in it to cheer you up and give you hope." For in the very same scroll which has the description of a man being castrated, just a bit further on, there is the promise of the prophet.

'A man who has been castrated should never think that because he cannot have children he can never be part of God's people.'
(Isaiah 56)

Maybe the prophet was talking from his own experience. He wrote to give hope for the future for all those, like him, who had been through this terrible trauma.

So Philip preached to the Ethiopian's situation. You may have been rejected by the Temple and by the Jewish religion, but God has not rejected you. Jesus, God's Chosen, has come to announce the inclusion of everybody in God's New World. We are building a new church without walls, a new community in which barriers of place of origin and colour and sex have been done away with, and everybody is welcome. "Are you telling me I am eligible to join your church?", asks the castrated man. "Of course," says Philip. "Well then, I'm ready. What about this oasis we're just coming to? Will it do?"

Jesus' teaching about eunuchs. What is a eunuch today?

'..there are eunuchs who have been so from birth, and there are eunuchs who have been made eunuchs by others, and there are eunuchs who have made themselves eunuchs for the sake of the kingdom of heaven..' (Matthew 19:12)

Jesus's friends said to him, "You're making marriage sound very difficult. Perhaps it would be better not to get married." Jesus said, "It is difficult for some people. Marriage is a special relationship for those suited to it. Marriage is not right for certain types. It may be just the way they are, or something to do with how they've been brought up. Sometimes people choose to avoid close personal attachments so they can give their full time to help bring in The Bright New World. We must be understanding of one another."
(Good As New)

Jesus addressed the question of eunuchs in the context of the ill-treatment of women. It is amazing how the churches have turned this passage into one which allows them to make strict rulings about marriage and divorce. (verses 10 & 11), missing the whole point. The male disciples were worried about whether, in view of Jesus' urging greater care for the humanity and sensitivity of their wives, it would be better not to get married at all. They were not up to such a leap in culture. Jesus's reply is that being a 'eunuch' is an acceptable option. Jesus believed in options. It is up to the reader to decide whether Jesus was talking about a eunuch in the castrated sense, or, in view of the context, a man (or even a woman) who decides not to marry either out of personal preference or because it leaves them free to love and serve a wider constituency. Or indeed was Jesus setting forth liberal principles and attitudes which his followers would be free to interpret (or go back on) in other times and cultures.

It is highly likely that Philip the Good News Vendor was influenced not only by the passages in the prophet(s) of the exile but by the teaching of Jesus which was in tune with those passages. After all, these scriptures seem to have been favourites of Jesus. He was influenced by the ideal of the Servant of God they portrayed. It may be that the so-called 'Twelve' ignored his teaching on relationships and their variety, just as they did his approach to the Gentiles . (Both depended greatly on the Book of Isaiah, much of which can be seen as the New Testament/ Covenant in the Hebrew Scriptures.) Some gay people see these verses as Jesus' okay to the 'gay' option, and they are right to do so, even though the orientation as we understand it was not recognized in Jesus' day, neither were the many other orientations we put under the microscope. No doubt it all went on in his day if you knew where to look for it.

However there are many today, gay, straight or something else, who do not wish to be hitched legally or sacramentally to a partner. Jesus says they have a right to that option. They may wish to cultivate a circle of friends, some perhaps with the option of sexual expression of friendship from time to time, or not as the case may be. Some gay Christian leaders are very opposed to such an idea. Gays must parallel straights in their mores. "We have found our exclusive life partner with whom we are happy. We're all right, Jack! Everybody else must do the same, or we will cause them grief the way straights used to cause it to us." (Jesus had a parable about that sort of thing.)

There are others who are natural loners. I've always had a problem with this, since I am not a loner, despite valuing my periods alone. But the loner wishes to maximise their aloneness, and to live in close proximity with someone else perpetually would be hell. There are eunuchs who may medically be eunuchs, from birth, or by accident in the work place, doing sports, or on military service. And there are priests who take vows of celibacy, presumably as a means of taking Jesus words about 'eunuchs for the kingdom' seriously, though rarely I would think these days by being castrated. This vow we know only too well is not always kept. There is confession and forgiveness. There are also people who naturally have a low sex drive. Perhaps they make good priests, but only in my opinion because Jesus accepts all sorts. The Church does not concern itself sufficiently how we show love to the physically sexually disabled or those who for whatever reason find it difficult to find a partner and may never do so. And even the loner enjoys having a birthday card or present – or so I have found.

Why, O why, O why, cannot we just rejoice in the Good News that in the matter of sexuality or lack of it, God loves us, accepts us, needs us and recruits us all. We are to love, honour, respect all those whom God has made. We are not to hurt or abuse. Telling others who and how and under what conditions they should love, is a form of abuse.

Amazing, isn't it, that two thousand years ago Philip befriended and baptized someone whose sexuality did not fit the norm. In the third Millennium it is still considered way-out for a Christian minister to argue his cause!

CHAPTER FOURTEEN

SAME SEX
AND THE BIBLE

Homosexuality and the Bible – *being a lecture John Henson gave many times in the late 1980s/early 1990s. 'I have included this mostly unchanged. Much work has been done on this topic since I wrote this lecture. But I believe that what I thought in those days is still worth having a look at.'*

First, something about the Bible. Christians differ greatly in the place they give the Bible as a source of authority for Christian behaviour. There are those who believe the Bible to be the 'Word of God' in the sense that every word, every letter, every dot and comma is literally true, inerrant and to be obeyed absolutely. These are 'Fundamentalists'. There are those who regard the Bible as a unique record of the relationship between

God and people throughout many centuries, with varying perceptions of God's truth, limited by time and culture, and subject to human error. Paul says Jesus Christ is the one and only foundation for the Christian faith (1 Corinthians 3:13). The Bible is important because it is one of the witnesses to him. But it is Jesus himself who is 'The Word of God', 'God Speaking'(John 1:1)

The Bible has very little to say on the subject of homosexuality considering how large a collection of books the Bible is. There are perhaps twelve references at most. What there is has been twisted and misused to serve the purposes of homophobia in much the same way that a few scanty texts were in the past used to uphold racism. Those who persecute gay people do not gain their inspiration from the Bible and certainly not from Jesus who blessed the persecuted. Their mindset is closer to that of Hitler.

THE HEBREW SCRIPTURES

The Old Testament means the old relationship between God and God's people based on the law given to Moses at Mount Sinai. But the first key passage comes from a time before the law was given. This is the story of Sodom, Genesis 19: 1-11. The homophobic interpretation of this story is that it condemns the sin of homosexuality for which Sodom was destroyed by a volcano. However, since this is before the time of Moses, we have no means of telling whether homosexuality at that time was regarded as sinful or not. What we do know about Middle-Eastern culture at that time and throughout history is the importance placed on hospitality. Two attractive men, identified by Abraham as angel-messengers, were visitors to the city, guests of Lot, Abraham's nephew. The attempt of a gang to rape them was an extreme abuse of hospitality. It is significant that when Jesus mentions Sodom and Gomorrah (Matthew 10: 11-15) he does so when he is talking about transgression of the customs of hospitality. If we are to understand what God is saying to us in this scripture today we should relate it to our treatment of immigrants and asylum seekers and indeed any type of person who strikes us as strange or different.

There have been incidents on the London underground of gay men being raped by gangs of heterosexual men in the same way as was proposed by the men of Sodom. It is just possible that this is the scenario of Sodom – an attack by macho thugs on those they thought to be effeminate because of their good looks. Fear, envy and ignorance are displayed – the regular cocktail of homophobia!

The next oft-quoted text is Leviticus 18:22 [cf. Lev. 20:13 & Deut. 20:13 a ban on prostitution, male & female] This is part of the Law of Holiness for the Israelite people and was a filling out of the basic set of rules embodied in the ten commandments. Probably it is meant to be understood as a ban on anal intercourse, (or on a man adopting a feminine posture)- the literal meaning of the text which is just one of a variety of acts by which some (not all) gay men express their affection for one another. The rule was a wise piece of advice in a hot climate without any modern methods of protection or drugs to clear infections. The onset of AIDS has brought the advice very up-to-date. The Israelites were marching through the desert, a prey to hostile races. Their prime concern was for a strong, healthy fighting force. Proper attention to hygiene must still be a prime concern in any responsible relationship, gay or straight. We now have more exact knowledge of how viruses and bacteria attack the body. AIDS has taught us we cannot just rely on cures; prevention is the first concern. More recently the view has been put forward that Leviticus 8:22 has to do with a ban against the rape of a male. According to the culture and customs of the time, the rape of female prisoners of war was universal. Often the male prisoners were included in this rape as a form of subjugation and humiliation. The law then is restricting the degree of rape allowed, exempting males from being recipients. The rape of females in war has remained customary in many countries to this day. The rape of men is still not unknown and American soldiers were captured on camera sexually abusing male prisoners in the war in Iraq. There is some suspicion that UK soldiers may also have perpetrated the same kind of abuse. It goes without saying that all this has nothing to do with affectionate and responsible relationships between people of the same sex.

The laws of Leviticus were meant for the Jewish people at a certain period. Anyone who uses this text as a ban for all time must logically be prepared to keep all the other laws of Leviticus. (e.g. 19:27 "Do not cut the hair at the sides of your beard or clip off the edges of your beard.") I do not know any Christian who even tries to keep all the rules in Leviticus. Paul makes it clear throughout his letters that Christians have been set free from the bondage of the Law. (See especially Galatians 3: 10-12)

DAVID AND JONATHAN
(1 SAMUEL CHAPTERS 18-20)

The story of David and Jonathan is the most obvious and explicit account of a gay relationship in the Bible. There is no sense anywhere in the text that their love for one another and its physical expression is disapproved of by God – quite the reverse. The story begins by telling us that David and Jonathan are bound 'soul to soul' as the result of a brief encounter. This is 'love at first sight', not something that happens very often, but we recognize it when it does, and it is easily recognized in the scriptural account. Jonathan expresses his feelings by dressing David in his own clothes. (18;4) Jonathan is described as 'taking great delight' in David (19:1), and in 'loving David as his own soul.' (18:3 & 20:17) At their parting they kiss and weep. (20:41) No translation that has the official approval of the Church is prepared to translate the Hebrew explicitly. David is described as 'exceeding himself' and translations dodge this in various ways. The Hebrew is 'higdil' which means to swell up and suggests that David had an erection (or an ejaculation).

What clinches it is the attitude of King Saul, Jonathan's father, to the relationship. He indulges in a typical homophobic outburst from an outraged parent. (1 Sam; 20:30)

"You son of a perverse, rebellious woman! Do I not know that you have chosen the son of Jesse to your own shame, and to the shame of your mother's nakedness?"

Saul typically blames the influence of Jonathan's mother for his perversity. But we must note that, at this stage in the story, Saul has been possessed by an evil spirit and God has already chosen David to replace him. God approves David's love for Jonathan. God does not approve of the way Saul spits on the love of others. No-one with an open mind today, reading this story for the first time could have any doubt that David and Jonathan had what we would describe as a gay relationship and that whoever wrote the story down thought it a good thing.

THE CHRISTIAN SCRIPTURES

The New Testament material of interest is mainly to be found in the letters of Paul. Paul gives us his background in Philippians 3:5 ' a Hebrew born and bred; in my attitude to the law, a Pharisee,..in legal rectitude, faultless." That is, Paul began his spiritual career with some dreadful hang-ups and admitted it! He concludes this autobiographical sketch (v70) by writing it all off in favour of Christ. Paul showed great courage in rejecting his background. He made a bold stand against the 'circumcisers'. These were Christians who continued to insist on obedience to the laws of Moses.

There seems little doubt that Paul disapproved of homosexuality as he perceived it in his day. For that matter he did not approve of any sex very much. (1 Cor. 7:25-40) However had he been alive today he may well have championed gay rights in the same way he controversially and courageously championed rights for the uncircumcised. In Paul's day gay rights were not on the agenda.

Paul was not only influenced by his background as a Pharisee, which would have bound him to Leviticus, but by his experience of homosexuality in the Greek/Roman world. It was frequently associated with the idol worship of the pagan temples. Temple prostitution was still part of pagan worship. Often the prostitutes were boys. The idea of worshipping God in this way was more than any Jew or Christian could stomach.

ROMANS 1: 18-32

This is the introduction to Paul's great theological work in which he sets out God's plan of salvation. Chapter 1 deals with the sinfulness of the Gentiles, chapter 2 with that of the Jews. Chapter 1:18-32 is very largely a description of pagan worship and the morality that springs from it. Idolatry and immoral practices go together. In vs. 26-27 Paul includes lust as between one man and another (and female/female or female/male? –it is not quite clear) It is lust Paul is condemning – the use of one person by another simply to promote their own aims and wishes.

There is no explicit mention of sex. The word 'unnatural' refers to the unnaturalness of idolatry, which turns God into an object. It is similarly unnatural to treat other people as things, whether as 'sex objects' or opponents in the gladiatorial contests in the arena which led to mutilation or death. It is also possible that Paul is referring to the way in which Roman soldiers frequently sexually abused their male captives. Paul's disgust at such practices can hardly be used as a guide to what he would have to say to a responsible and caring gay relationship. Paul is not talking about sex as an expression of affection. We must agree with him that all human relating is spoilt by sin, that is selfishness. Paul will go on to say this means that our salvation comes not by way of a return to legalism but by trusting in the grace, mercy and forgiveness of God that we receive as a free gift through Jesus. Everything leads to 8:1. (See next chapter for a fuller study of this scripture.)

1 CORINTHIANS 6:1-11

Here again homosexuality occurs in the context of paganism. Paul is addressing past pagans who are in danger of slipping back into their old ways, including pursuing each other in the courts. (Nobody says much about this!) Some of them may previously have been temple prostitutes, or have used them. The two words Paul uses have often been translated in a homophobic way – 'homosexuals' or even 'perverts'. The Greek terms are more specific. 'Malakoi' is probably the technical term for prostitutes and 'arsenokoitoi' for pederasts (users of young boys). Both refer to those who engage in anti-social or abusive behaviour. There is nothing here to prohibit relationships between consenting adults on the basis of genuine affection. (The same is true of 1 Timothy 1:8-10 (esp. v.10) where arsenokoitai is used in the context of breaches of the civil law.)

None of this enables us to say that Paul was a champion of homosexuality. But it is possible for us to imagine him coming to different conclusions in a different age and with greater knowledge.

Romans 14:14 (and Titus 1:5) Paul offers an important principle, relevant to this debate. "To the pure, all things are pure." "I know and am persuaded in the Lord Jesus that nothing is unclean in itself; but it is unclean for anyone who thinks it unclean." Paul is referring to food, but the principle can be applied generally. Here we have Paul at the edge of his radicalism, – the Paul who likes to leave issues open so that the Spirit of Jesus is given a chance to speak. (Cf. Romans 13:8-10 – "Love is the fulfilling of the law.")

THE GOSPELS

The gospels are the record of the words and deeds of Jesus. Jesus, our true foundation, says nothing on the subject of homosexuality. Nothing can be argued from silence. We know nothing of the sexuality of Jesus with any certainty- whether he was married or whether he was homosexual, bisexual, heterosexual or asexual. (Maybe we never will know. Maybe there are some areas in which there is a right of eternal privacy.) What we do know is that Jesus loved men and women passionately and physically. Mary Magdala had a special relationship with him, as did a male disciple who is described as 'the disciple Jesus loved' (For his true identity simply read John 11 carefully!) Jesus did not just have a vague love for humanity – he loved people individually and personally. He expressed these loves physically in allowing a prostitute to give him a massage, in washing the feet of the disciples and in lying close to the beloved disciple at the Last Supper. The customary way of greeting his friends was with a kiss.

Although we have no indisputable example of Jesus including gay people in his proclamation of 'good news', the whole bias of his ministry was towards those who were outcasts and referred to as 'sinners' by the religious of the day. These included prostitutes, lepers, the mentally ill, foreigners, women, terrorists, traitors, criminals and other non-respectable people. The way he mixed and even ate with such people was a scandal to the righteous.

THE ROMAN CENTURION

The Roman centurion mentioned in the gospels expected Jesus to disapprove of his life style, because he knew what the other religious leaders thought. He did not want Jesus to go to his house. Perhaps there were statues of naked men in the dining room or pornographic pictures. He didn't want to embarrass Jesus. Jesus healed his boyfriend, however and gave the centurion a pat on the back. We are not told the sequel to the story, but it is difficult to imagine Jesus not going back home with him afterwards. It is inconceivable that the man did not become a Christian once the church got going.

'Pais' in the Matthew account as 'boyfriend'. It can mean child, male or female, buddy or mate, or boyfriend in the sense of a sexual partner. Matthew does not, like Luke in his version (chap 7) use the less ambiguous 'doulos' = slave. 'Houseboy' is a compromise that covers both Matthew and Luke's understanding of the situation.

John confuses (or elucidates?) the situation by using 'huios'= son; 'pais'= child/mate and; 'paidion'= an affectionate form of 'pais' suggestive of something other than a father/son relationship. It was expression used by Jesus to his Galilean fishermen friends, John 21

Slowly, but slowly, New Testament scholars are coming to admit, one by one, that the man of whom Jesus said, "I have not found such faith, no not in Israel" was gay. It was very common in the Roman army for a subordinate to double as a sexual partner. The Emperor Augustus was a bit of a puritan and tried to put a stop to it. But by the time of Jesus Tiberius was Emperor and he enjoyed homosexuality himself, so did nothing to discourage gay sex among the troops.

THE SYRIAN WOMAN

The view of Ched Myers, a notable N.T. scholar in the States is that the Syrian Woman of Mark 7: 24 was Lesbian. If so it makes an interesting partner story with the story of the centurion. Both were foreigners and worshipped other gods, which was bad enough. In Mark it is not the normal word for her unwell girl, 'thugater', but an affectionate form 'thugaterion' which could be translated 'girl friend'. There is no suggestion of a husband or that the woman was a widow. Her confidence in taking on a man in a theological debate and winning – to Jesus' delight, suggests at least that she was a women's libber.

So those who prefer Paul to Jesus because they think Paul offers them a basis for their homophobia, should be warned that Paul may not turn out to be the comfort they think. Paul was against lust. Lust means any way of treating someone with less than the full respect due to someone made in the image of God. Homophobia is a form of lust. Gay people often say 'Jesus said nothing about homosexuality'. He said a lot about the sins of the Pharisees. However, we ought now to say 'Jesus said nothing about gay sexual relations, but it looks very much as if he was friendly with gay people.'

JESUS' LOVE FOR MEN

Only in the case of three men is Jesus actually described as loving an individual, though he showed loving actions to many men and women. These were (i) The disciple Jesus loved of John's Gospel (ii) The rich young ruler Mark 10:21 and (iii) Lazarus. – John 11:3 & 35. They are more than likely the same person. It means that contemporaries of Jesus noticed looks, smiles, actions between Jesus and another man, or men, which they considered worth commenting about and recording. None of this means a homosexual relationship as we understand it today or that Jesus was 'gay'. But what is homosexuality? Basically it is an affectionate relationship between two people of the same sex. Ask most Christians what is wrong with that and they will probably say, "Well, that's alright. What we regard as sinful is what homosexuals do." This leads on to the real problem.

THE REAL PROBLEM

The real problem is that it is not homosexuality that is the basic hang-up among Christians but sex. This author was brought up as a protestant puritan to believe that sex was exclusively for the procreation of children. I thought my parents had only had sex once, since they had only produced one child. I was quite shocked when later in my teens I encountered the view that sex could be enjoyed for its own sake and was a means of expressing affection between two people. This hang-up is part of the ancient Gnostic heresy, very prevalent in the early Church, which believed that the spirit was good and the flesh evil, to the extent that the true incarnation of Christ was denied because that would involve him in evil. After two thousand years Christians still have negative feelings about sex, which prevents them from enjoying it as a gift of God. The Church's panic about the gay experience is simply the sharp end of these old negative feelings. These feelings have coloured all the passages in the Bible where sex or affectionate feelings are mentioned. We look at the Bible to find confirmation of our judgemental and censorious views. When Christians finally get over their hang-up about sex they will find that the Bible is not so unfriendly towards a variety of sexual expression as was previously supposed. Gay Christian people are performing an important service in obliging the Church to re-think its whole attitude to sex. It is proving a very painful experience for many. But the gay experience is part of a discovery of the twentieth century that sex is a valid means of expressing affection apart from the impulse to reproduce. This may prove to be the great revelation of God's Spirit to the age. But it begins with the incarnation of Jesus and the recognition of him as a true human being. The Incarnation is God's stamp of approval on human flesh. Human flesh is good, human flesh is beautiful, human flesh is desirable, the chosen vehicle of the love of God and the proper vehicle for our loves.

I am constantly dismayed when I meet gay people who tell me they are not Christian because the Bible forbids homosexuality. What has happened is that at some point in their career a Christian has opened the Bible in front of their nose, pointed to a text and said, "There you are, you're out!" Whereas if they had examined the scriptural passages more closely they might have come to the conclusion that the Bible was being used as a tool of a particularly nasty prejudice.

CHAPTER FIFTEEN

CRACKING ROMANS 1-2

Romans chapters 1& 2 should not be separate chapters but should be read together. (There are no chapters at all in the original Greek text.)

ROMANS 1: 18

God's fierce opposition has been declared against all the evil and wickedness done by people who shamefully suppress the truth. Everything it's possible to know about God has been made known to humankind – God has made sure of that. Though God's character is too wonderful for us to understand, from the beginning of time it's been easy to grasp something of it through the world of nature. There's no excuse for complete ignorance! Though people can tell what God is like, they take no notice. They aren't grateful for God's gifts. Instead they've filled their minds with nonsense and gone wandering down every dark alley. They thought they were being clever while making fools of themselves. In the place of God who lives forever, they put statues of people, who live for no time at all, or even animals, birds or snakes. God has watched them go on from this to despise one another and to practice all kinds of abuse. Because they've twisted the truth about God, their attitude to the material world is twisted too. They've forgotten that the source of lasting good is God, not things! God let them go on to pursue their selfish desires. Women use their charms to further their own ends. Men, instead of being friends, ruthlessly exploit one another. Their stressful life-style makes them ill.

When people have no interest in getting to know what God is really like, God has no option but to leave them to their own evil thoughts, which lead to every kind of inhuman conduct. There is no end to their wickedness. Such people are greedy and envious, they commit murder, they quarrel and deceive; they play dirty tricks, they gossip and slander one another; they hate the very idea of God; they're arrogant, with no respect for their parents; they're silly, unreliable, lacking any tender feelings or scruples. They know they're offending God and that they don't deserve to live. Yet not only do they persist in their evil ways, they encourage others to do the same. (2:1) But you've no excuse either, if you think you're in a position to criticize other people, because your critical attitude shows you're as bad as they are. We know God is a fair judge when people behave badly. Do you think when you criticize other people for behaving in the same way as you do, it will somehow put God off the scent? Shouldn't you be more appreciative of God's kindness, patience and tolerance in your own case? Don't you realize that God's kindness is intended to get you to change your frame of mind? But your hard, unbending attitude means you're going to be in for *a nasty shock on the day God's fair judgment is announced. God will take into account the whole pattern of your life. To those who have patiently tried to be a permanent influence for good, God will give life to the full; while for those who've been selfish and ignore the truth about their own wickedness, the consequences will be unpleasant in the extreme.'* etc. (GOOD AS NEW)

This is a key text for homophobes. It is a good example of need to translate 'contextually' if we are to avoid fundamentalist errors. Fundamentalists and Undermentalists prefer 'texts' to the 'text'. I hope we have translated in such a way that for the first time ever ordinary Christians can read Romans and follow Paul's argument right through.

Paul's model for chapters one and two of Romans was the prophet Amos. Amos was a prophet from Judah who prophesied to Israel. (Judah and Israel at the time were separate rival states, but they had much the same religion). Amos begins his prophesy by bashing one by one the bad behaviour of all the non-Jewish states around. He does a tour of the little world of those days. (Read Amos 1: v.8 on) Then he turns to Judah – closer to home, Jewish, but another 'denomination' (2: 4) You can see his hearers getting more and more righteously indignant as the sins of all these other people are paraded. We must imagine Amos pausing for a breath. Then he goes biff, bang, wallop "For three sins of ISRAEL and for four" v. 6. Amos has been playing on the false spiritual pride of God's people in order to knock them off their own shaky pedestals.

You cannot understand Romans 1 unless you read Romans 2. In Romans 1 Paul parades the sins of the Gentiles, especially idolatry, playing on his own people's prejudices and self-righteousness. Chapter two begins, (NIV) "You, therefore, have no excuse, you who pass judgement on someone else..." Paul obviously knew the words of Jesus, "Judge not, that you be not judged." The most serious sin of all is to usurp God's prerogative of judgement. That is the most extreme form of idolatry. Paul is on his way to the assertion "All have sinned" – we are all in the same boat. And then on to "There is now no condemnation to those who are in Christ Jesus." Being 'in Christ Jesus" includes being like Jesus – non-judgemental. Engage in judgement and you step outside of Jesus.

Let's have a closer look at the words used to bash people over the head with

v. 18 'wrath' is a seventeenth century translation. It belongs to the days when authority expressed its disapproval by torturing people. It should never be forgotten that the authors of the KJV, including James I who traslated some of the psalms, were in favour of burning witches..The prime meaning of the Greek orge (οργη) is attitude or disposition. God is not an angry, bad tempered, out of control Tudor or Stuart monarch. God is against wrongdoing, especially the ill treatment of one person by another. Paul is going to outline God's plan for doing away with such wickedness, which is not by bashing people over the head, but by a demonstration of God's everlasting love in the cross and the Resurrection of Jesus.

Using Amos' technique Paul relates how the peoples of the world (apart from the Jews of course) have worshipped idols – statues- instead of the living God. They have turned God into 'things'. There is a direct link between this and the fact that they go on to treat other people as 'things'. The words that follow have been traditionally translated to give the impression that it is homosexual acts Paul is referring to. In fact there is NO specific mention of homosexual acts in the text whatsoever. You can argue about the meaning of the Greek until the cows come home. The only thing that is obvious is that Paul is talking about the ill treatment of one person by another. People are being treated as objects instead of as living beings. That is unnatural in the same way that it is unnatural not to perceive through the world of nature that God is a living being, not a thing, not an object to be manipulated for our own convenience.

Paul may well have had in mind the sexual exploitation of prostitutes in the heathen temples. It's just as likely he also had in mind the gladiatorial contests in the Roman arenas. In both cases people were physically and mentally wounded, and those who enjoyed the experience degraded. There is more than one way of abusing another. Paul has quite a list.

According to the New International Version it includes 'greed' –when did your Church last expel a member for being greedy? Strife? We don't have that in our churches do we? Arrogant? None of that in our fellowships is there? Gossips? And at the beginning of chapter two – judgemental, because when you judge someone you fail to treat them as a real person. You treat them as an object of your opinion.

NOTE ON KEY GREEK WORDS

'παθη' = feelings; 'ατιμιας' = very bad, negative; taken together = nasty feelings. NB The type of feelings is not specified.

'θηλεια' (=women) 'μετηλλαξαν' (=exhange) 'φυσικην χρισιν' (=natural role) into that 'παραφυσιν' (=against nature) Paul probably means that instead of fulfilling the normal role of the Jewish mother and housekeeper, women are competing in the man's world by following careers in entertainment, the service industries or business. There is nothing about women doing anything sexy with one another!

'αρρενες' (=men) 'αφεντες' (=abandoning) 'φυσικην χρησιν' (=natural role) 'της θηλειας' (towards women.) For Paul the Jew, the natural role of men towards women was that of protector and respecter of their weaker composition , as in those days assumed.

They ie. men 'εξεκαυθησαν' (=burn) in 'ορεξει' (=general word for any kind of feelings, desire, intention) 'εις αλληλους' (= towards one another) 'αρσενες εν αρσεσι' (men in relationship to other men). They 'κατεργαζομενοι' (=perpetuate) 'ασχημοσυνην' (=shameful or dishonourable acts).

It is necessary to have a mind predisposed in a certain direction in order to be absolutely convinced that Paul is talking about sex. If Paul had wished to be more precise, he would have been moreprecise, as in 1 Corinthians 6:9, where he uses technical terms for sexual offenders and abusers of the young. One would have expected him at the very least to include the word 'σαρχ' (flesh), if he was talking about physical acts. Paul is simply talking about men being beastly to one another, in whatever way. A viewing of the film 'Gladiator' will give some idea of what he means.

They 'απολαμβανοντες' (=receive) 'εν εαυτοις' (in themselves) 'αντιμισθιαν εν εδει' (the just reward or inevitable consequence) of their 'πλανης' (going astray, bad/stupid behaviour.) Again, see the Gladiator to find out what happens to men who ill treat one another!

We must say something about the word 'paraphusin' 'παραφυσιν'. (= against nature or 'unnatural'). Strangely in this passage, Paul uses the idea of 'natural' as if it were something good, whereas more often in his writings he believes it to be something bad, contrasting 'natural' with 'spiritual'. This should alert us to the danger of jumping to conclusions when Paul uses this term. In context, as we have seen, it means to treat God or other humans as objects. It may also be that Paul's usage approximates to our use of such words as 'frightful', 'awful', 'appalling' when in fact we are not frightened, awed, or covered by a pall!

Natural Law theology was not developed until the Middle Ages and Paul would not have understood it. Paul's Jewish ethics from his training as a Pharisee were based on what God tells you to do or not to do in the Torah, not on shaky notions of what is natural or unnatural. A contemporary idea of 'natural' as 'at ease with oneself' or 'act natural' might be a possible way of translating for the future.

CHAPTER SIXTEEN

THE UNITY OF THE SEXUALITIES

John said, "Boss, we saw someone who doesn't belong to us healing people by using your name, and we tried to put a stop to it." But Jesus said, "That was wrong of you. You should have recognized someone like that as your ally."

(Luke 9: 49. Good As New page 204.)

While going for a walk along a beach in South Wales with Peterson Toscano, Peterson asked me a question. "John, do you think someone can change from 'Gay' to 'Straight' or 'Straight' to 'Gay'? My reply resulted in a 3 or 4 point sermon, some of which I will now try to report to you.

Firstly, Gay and straight (with the addition of bi-sexual, transgendered etc) are not the only categories the human psyche may be divided into, nor for many people are they the most important categories. A more important one for many people would be the categories 'conventional' or 'unconventional'. For many people the most important thing in their lives is to conform to and therefore be accepted by the society or the sub-society in which they find themselves. Only thus can they feel comfortable. They can even chameleon-like adapt when they move from one culture to another, after an initial period of discomfort. Thus even if their sexuality falls well on the homosexual end of the line, they will adapt to a heterosexual life-style if that is the prevailing norm. They will have gay fantasies, they may have the odd gay encounter of which they feel ashamed or amused, but they will marry, have two kids, a mortgage and a car, like almost everybody else. Others are natural rebels, they will constantly be trying to break out of whatever confinements they find themselves in, they will adventure personally and they will shock socially. They may join a hippy commune, experiment with drugs or sex. Even if they are basically heterosexual they will do their best to be in touch with their feminine side, and *just because* the prevailing society tells them gay is not the thing to be, they will have a go at it, or at least be ostentatiously supportive of gay friends. They may well find that gay sex is not difficult to enjoy. I liked the banner held aloft by one woman on a gay pride march. "I'm heterosexual. But maybe it's only a phase!" It is important to realise that for someone for whom conventionality or unconventionality is more important than sexual orientation, trying to be unconventional or conventional if it is not their thing is more uncomfortable than trying to display the wrong sexuality. In many cases, of course, conflicts will arise between the two competing tensions.

This is heresy to orthodox gay theology. There is a gay fundamentalism which says gays must be gays and straights must be straight, they were made that way, it's in the genes, and they cannot change. Until quite recently there was considerable resistance amongst gays to the idea that someone could be bi-sexual. It was thought to be messing about. Bi-sexual was 'a homosexual on a bicycle'. According to gay fundamentalism, the most important thing in life is that you get your sexuality sorted out, get into the right box and stay there. I think there are many other important things in life competing with this imperative. I spent twelve years, from 'O' levels to my Oxford degree, preparing for and taking exams, catching up, since I had failed the 11 plus. This period included 7 years at university. For the whole twelve 12 years I was celibate, despite the fact that I already had some experience. Something inside me told me very strongly that if I were to succeed academically- which I was desperate to do -, I had to avoid entanglements. I managed it *just*, disappointing friends of both sexes on the way. But I could not keep putting my career first in that way for a lifetime. Some people do. They put business before pleasure – sexual pleasure at any rate.

Secondly, let's think about sexuality. We have got used to the idea that there is a line with 99 per cent gay at one end and 99 per cent straight at the other, and that we are all at different points along that line, though we are not yet quite used to the idea that people can move along the line. But the line from gay to straight is not the only line that affects our sexuality. There is a line between 'highly sexed' and 'under-sexed'. I believe that where you are on this line is just as important a consideration as whether you are predominantly gay or straight. And, of course, you can move along this line too. Someone who is very highly sexed requires sex badly and requires it often. If there is no partner of the preferred sexuality, sometimes needs must that they find satisfaction in the alternative. It may be that it is more convenient, and less expensive perhaps, to go for the alternative option, especially if a partner or partners are available who are more than willing. In the eighties when for a time in Soho gay sex parlours with brightly advertized frontage competed with their girlie equivalent, they attracted straight men requiring a quick thrill simply because they were considerably less expensive and less predatory. You were not obliged to buy an over-priced drink, for example. There are other lines of sexuality we could talk about. The line with 'dominant' at one end and 'likes to be dominated at the other'; or (not quite the same) 'active' and 'passive', or 'gentle' and vigorous', or 'strictly monogamous' and 'extremely polygamous', or 'guilt-ridden and 'carefree', fussy about clothes or hygiene and not fussy at all, tied to a particular age-range, colour, body shape, absence or presence of hair, or not so tied. You may be able to think of some more. Sexuality is not a line, it's a patchwork quilt!

Thirdly, there are many people for whom companionship is more important than sex. To have as a friend, someone with the same interests, ideals, religious faith as their partner is better than someone who fulfils their sexual requirements to a tee, but with whom otherwise they have little or nothing in common. Many people put up with, if those are the right words, a mediocre sex life, because in other respects they have the ideal partner. Once a husband and wife came to me for counselling. They had been together for many years, loved one another very deeply, were very happy and yet had never had sex because neither of them fancied it. Was one of them or both of them gay? I've no idea. I think it was irrelevant. I think also there are people who choose a friend, not because that friend is the opposite sex or the same sex, but because they like them and get on with them. I have a friend who recently retired as a research scientist. He was married when a post graduate student to a very beautiful woman, making his colleagues quite envious. Two years later he came home from the lab to find a note on the table which simply said 'I have left you'. He had had no warning. He thought he had a very happy marriage. He never saw his wife again. He was devastated, and had a breakdown. Much of the rest of his life was spent with one female partner after another. They all turned out to be unpleasant women. He didn't seem very good in the matter of making choices. I had lunch with him shortly after he retired. He said, "I've done with women. They were a disaster for me. I've found myself a nice man and we're getting on fine!" Some of his other friends have said to me, "That means he was gay all along and only now has owned up to it." But I don't think so. I think I know him better. He had the hots for his wife alright and for his other women. He just had a bad time with them. Again this is heresy to gay fundamentalists, but I think that some people go gay or straight (sometimes only for a while) because they meet someone nice who attracts them as a person. It is possible that some women who are abused by their husbands or male partners and then find the support they need from their female sisters, go over to being lesbian as a result of the contrast in their experience between the men who have treated them badly and the women who treated them well.

Fourthly, I think that the Christian Good News has a contribution to make to this debate about whether there is any element of choice in our relationship with our own or the opposite sex. In his life and ministry Jesus demonstrated his ancestry from God and from Jacob in his revolutionary approach to women and in the integration of the feminine with the masculine in his own character and behaviour. Jesus made all classes of the oppressed his priority targets, including women. Luke makes it quite clear in Chapter 8 that Jesus had female as well as male disciples.

The way Jesus mixed easily and freely with women was a source of astonishment to his followers. They were surprised to find him talking to Tina, the woman of Samaria,, at the well (Jn.4). Both were unaccompanied – scandalous behaviour by the standards of the day. Prostitutes were among the bad company Jesus kept and brought the scorn of his critics the Pharisees (e.g. Mk. 15:1). According to Jesus, prostitutes would arrive in God's New World before the God Squad. (Mat.21:31)

Jesus showed the same kind of freedom in his dealings with other men as he did in his dealings with women. John's Gospel contains frequent references to a man referred to as 'the disciple Jesus loved'. The straightforward explanation is that there was a man who Jesus loved more strongly and more intensely than the rest of his friends and that this was an open secret to those who knew him well. Because of the problems Christians have about two people of the same sex loving one another, they try to imagine a not very convincing relationship devoid of any physical, sexual or intensely emotional aspects.

Scholars are now beginning to take seriously the possibility that Jesus was not silent on the question of same-sex relationships as people on all sides of the debate had supposed. Jesus sympathized with the centurion who expressed a strong love for his male servant. (Matt. 8:5ff) and also, less certain but possible, that he healed the partner of a lesbian Syrian woman.

Jesus was neither 'gay' nor a 'radical feminist' as we understand those terms nowadays. But I believe the gay experience and the feminist experience, which came so much to the fore at the end of the twentieth century, are a striving after what Jesus was aiming at. Both are incomplete answers to the problem of a humanity over-divided and stressed by the concepts of male and female. Gay liberation has been instrumental in giving all males extra options. Men, straight as well as gay, can now wear colourful clothes (including pink) and jewellery, use cosmetics and style their hair, if they choose.

But the aims of Jesus will not be attained whilst the divisions male, female, gay, straight cause people to huddle together in separate groups with rival and competing areas and life-styles. The aim of Jesus is for a society that holds within it the maximum variety of responsible and loving human expression, where each expression is regarded and valued by all as part of their common humanity. On the individual level, the aim of Jesus is for everyone to own and value those elements within themselves that they see expressed in others who may yet be very different from them. This means we may all have loving same-sex relationships and may all have loving relationships with the opposite sex, though what that entails will differ from relationship to relationship. But we shall all regard all types of relationship as an expression of the humanity we hold in common with others. There should be no need for ghettos created for the comfort and ease of specific types. We shall all be at ease and comfortable with one another. Though we do not seek a specific relationship, we shall be at one with those who do, and enter into their joy when they find it. Judgemental jealousy and envy will cease. God made us female and male. God also produced the rainbow. So the God who thought up red and yellow also thought up orange. If we deny this either within ourselves or within the society of which we are part, we are inadequate half-people. The purpose of God in Jesus is that male and female, gay and straight, etc and etc become one humanity 'the Complete Person'.

One day the temple of peace will live
in every human mind;
not far away on mountain tops,
but close at hand you'll find.

That peace will spread right round the globe
removing every trace
of hatred , anger and mistrust,
At last, one human race.

One day we'll wake to gentle strains
From war's horrotic trance;
we'll put our medals in a box,
and click our heels in dance.

No longer funerals in deepest black,
to honour yet more slain;
we'll roll our protest banners up
and not need them again.

The Prince of Peace will stroll among
The cheerful, grateful throng;
And former bitter enemies
Will join God's New World song.

(John Henson 18/10/15)

CHAPTER SEVENTEEN

MORE ABOUT LINES

THE MORAL LINE

For the Christian, and also those of other faiths, the most important line upon which people are based in respect of their potential behaviour, including their sexual behaviour, is 'The Moral Line'. That is the line from 'strong moral imperative' at one end to 'absence of any moral imperative' at the other end. Some might even wish to judge how good a Christian is with reference to where they are along this line, though others would remind us that we are 'saved by grace and justified through faith'. A moral imperative differs from a legal imperative where you do what you are told simply because you are told, without any deep thought or inner trauma as to why. Those with a moral imperative are agonizers and those who are Christian agonize above all as to whether they have the mind of

Christ, or behave in each situation as Jesus would behave. Thus anxiety not to cause another to stumble frequently enters the equation when a particular course of action is considered. This is because Jesus put forward the golden rule, 'Do unto others as you would have them do to you', a variation of the principle to 'love your neighbour as yourself'. It is possible both to refrain from sex and to engage in it under the impulse of this 'moral imperative'. It may not be the only consideration, probably isn't, but it may be the one that makes the difference.

THE PROMISCUITY LINE

In the sexuality debate as it is conducted by people with faith, or even with people without faith but with a strong moral imperative, you often reach a kind of uneasy, half-way conclusion, that okay we may have to accept gay people and gay partnership, we may even have to accept transgendered people and transvestites with their particular needs, but we must draw the line at promiscuity. The game of sex is to find a partner, enter a relationship, however unusual that relationship may be, and to stay there, committed, one to one, preferably for life. This is even seen as the churches' contribution to the debate. It is the imposition of order. We must draw the line somewhere. There must be no sleeping around. We can neither tolerate nor cope with 'anything goes'. The churches want to be able to pull themselves up to full stretch again and carry on as they always have, setting out the rules of engagement, instead of honestly getting to grips with the ethics. But here is a line we must learn to cope with and to consider from an ethical perspective, because it is a line that will always be there. It is the line from, at one end complete celibacy and at the other 'extreme promiscuity' (promiscuity limited only by time, space, energy and health.) We have heard many debaters on sexual ethics dismiss promiscuity as the ultimate immorality. The fact is that many people today practice a variety of forms of promiscuity and at the same time manage to be good people. This is nothing new. Many societies have accepted a degree of promiscuity in the practice of polygamy, including ancient Israel and modern Islam, chiefly, though not entirely, for the benefit of males and their overflowing needs. Women who take turns with others for their husband's attention, may also benefit by being spared excessive child bearing or sex when they have had enough of it. So a line can be found stretching from complete celibacy, through struggling celibacy, via the request stops of complete monogamy, and serial monogamy, to extended monogamy, selective promiscuity and extreme promiscuity. As with all lines, the extremes on either end are occupied by very few people. Towards one end there are those who like swans will not take another partner even if their partner dies, and at the other end the Cassanovas who require a new partner every time for adequate sexual fulfilment.

The first thing that has to be said from the Christian point of view, is that we are called to love our neighbour, and this includes Cassanova. The second is to learn that Christian ethics can be practised in situations that for many may seem bizarre. The third is to recognize that a great many people cannot be fitted into the one-to-one rule and never will be. A great many people do not manage to find a partner however hard they try. Others are unhappy with the partner they have, maybe have been unhappy for many years. Are we to say that someone is to be denied God's gift of sex with all its essential health-giving and therapeutic properties, simply because they cannot find someone willing to shack up with them for life? The churches seem to say 'Yes' with the implied overtones of 'tough' but God will give you strength to bear your misery, or 'You've made your bed with that person, you must lie on it'. Thus Christians become accused of inhumanity and making little effort to understand what life is all about for a lot of people.

Sex today, for many is a leisure activity, within or without a committed relationship or both. Like it or lump it, this is a fact of life in the 21st century. It is nothing new. Throughout my ministry I have come to hear of more and more stories of Baptist ministers of my parents' and grandparents' generation who had another partner 'on the side' in addition to their Christian marriage partner. All very carefully hushed up. Disaster if it came to light. More often than not it didn't. There was a conspiracy of silence. Lloyd George was an example of a man who could truly love and care for more than one person. It was never made public knowledge during his career in government. People made jokes about 'The Welsh Goat', but nothing got into the papers. He was far from being an unusual case. President Kennedy was notorius for having (surely an exaggeration) queues of women waiting at his door. Be that as it may, his promiscuity was legendary. Yet he is regarded as one of the USA's greatest presidents, and definetely one of the nicest.

In practice, sex takes place at a number of different levels. There is sex between committed partners, where the long-term relationship is the essential thing and sex the icing on the cake. Here we are inclined to see sex as at its highest expression, the expression of love as the assurance of continued loyalty and care and being together. Then friends of long standing or newer friends in the process of becoming valued, may have sex as an expression of their friendship. Some couples have friends, maybe mutual, maybe just a friend of one partner, whom they trust and see as no threat to their relationship if sex takes place outside the central relationship . Some may even have three-somes. Some deliberately make no commitment to their regular partner, in order to retain the freedom to friendship, including sex, with other friends. Some who do make a commitment, including those who make vows in church, also agree privately between themselves to an open relationship. This both caters for particular needs which one or other marriage partner may not be able to fulfil, and also may extend sex with accompanying love and care to someone who otherwise would not get it. Then there are those who have casual sex with those who are to all intents strangers, though they may bump into the same person now and again. This can sometimes turn out to be a genuine expression of friendship, friendship as it were just for the afternoon, but a genuine meeting and caring between two people. They may spend time in talk, discussing their lives and their problems. It may be a very small cup of love, but a cup of love nevertheless. Then there are those who will have sex with anybody at the drop of a hat, take little notice of them as a person, do not even ask their name, and will ignore them if they see them in the street next day. Just like going to the toilet with the assistance of somebody else! Even so, a release has been had, and that means that for two people the rest of the day may be less stressful. For Christians that kind of casual sex is likely to be highly unsatisfactory because someone is only used as an object and not seen as a brother or sister made in the image of God. But we must avoid words like 'sinful'. All these levels of sex can be positive and life-affirming providing there is genuine consent, the experience is friendly, free from abuse, and if there is consideration for the needs of the other and not just for self. For most I am daring to speak of pathways down which they have no intention of travelling. Good. As long as you do not think that your chosen style makes you more holy and less of a sinner than those whose style appears to be chaotic and risky. That goes against the central teaching of the gospel that 'all have sinned'. Whereas some may sin in expressing their love too widely, some may sin in not expressing it widely enough. God is our judge, not even ourselves of ourselves. Don't forget that God is promiscuous. I once said that to Liz Stuart and she repeated it the next week on the radio and got into a lot of trouble. But God is the only being who can love everybody and does. That sounds pretty promiscuous to me. My father, a Baptist minister and a saint, once said something to me which many find shocking when I repeat it to them. "My boy", he said, "I've come to the conclusion that it doesn't matter who goes to bed with whom. The only thing that matters is that people are kind to one another." You make shake your heads, but I think he was right.

I once attended a seminar at the Baptist Union Assembly of Great Britain, held in London. It was in the mid 1960s. This particular meeting took place in the Friendship Centre of Bloomsbury Baptist Church and was conducted by Ernest Payne, former Secretary of the Baptist Union, Church Historian, Christian Unity advocate , held in high honour among the Christian communities world-wide. He began by throwing out a question to those who had come to hear what he had to say. "What do you think are the most crucial issues facing the Christian Church today?" After one or two obvious things had been shouted out like 'Church Unity', 'decline in Church attendance', I shouted out "The Sexual Revolution". There was an uneasy silence that you could cut with a knife. Ernest Payne knew what I was talking about, but very few others did. Some were uncomfortable, even about the use of the word 'sexual' within the confines of a church. There was much discussion in society at that time about what was styled 'The New Morality', but insofar as it reached the pulpits it was usually condemned and dismissed scathingly as the old immorality. Christians, not for the first time in history, were missing the point. Ernie Payne wisely decided not to take up my challenge by accepting the topic I had given him for comment.

The Sexual Revolution is now almost complete in the 'advanced' western societies, though the 'emerging nations' are catching up quickly. The experimentation in thinking and practice in matters of sex during the second half of the twentieth century was truly exciting. Christians first stood aloof and aghast. Then, as they clung on tight to the pile of the carpet they were being sucked along by a gigantic vacuum cleaner. Holy Church occupied its thoughts and passions, and papal declarations, in trying to hold a fastly moving line. It's attitude to all change in this particular area was 99% negative. You know the story. Those of us who dared to suggest that God might to speaking through these developments, as God had once spoken through Christian people on such matters as the abolition of slavery and improved working conditions, were not understood. We were increasingly marginalized and denied a voice in pulpit and in Christian publications. In a way Christians were right to talk about the 'old immorality'. There is nothing new under the sun. Sexual freedoms had been practiced from time immemorial, especially during the 'puritanical' Victorian period when prostitution was rampant, much more so than today. But it was all under wraps, in secrecy and fear. Christians simply failed to pinpoint the immorality. The immorality was not sex but hypocrisy. This is still the case where sexual repression continues to be preached at many an evangelical mega-church, and all hold their breath wondering just when their golden good-looking idol of a preacher will be caught 'at it' . Nearly everybody knows, except the poor preacher it would seem, that those who have most to hide shout loudest.

So the Church has been badly left behind, still not thinking outside its box, still not ready to understand what has happened all around it. It still wants to pontificate, a minority with a majority complex, to a world that has done its thinking and exploring for it. The Church is still unwilling to realise it is time to shut up and to listen. The devils of misogyny and homophobia have been exorcised by those without Christian commitment. When I had my breakdown I was grateful that my psychiatrist was not a Christian. About midway through the twentieth century the churches said to themselves, "We don't like what seems to be going on in our society today, let's sing worship songs to ear splitting musak." They even managed to drown out the noise of the horrible wars that were taking place. Many Christians who wanted the freedom to follow Jesus, have stepped out into the world and left the Church behind. Others remain out of a sense of loyalty or hoping they can do something about it, but very uncomfortable. Count me as one.

What of the Church in the future? The writer of the Book of Revelation told us that there is to be no temple in the New Jerusalem. The people 'of the way' who first followed Jesus in the first century found that they did not need a temple. I may be a prophet, but I am not a clairvoyant. Maybe the Church will unite with other right-wing and repressive forces one day to destroy sexual freedom again, and other freedoms. Maybe the 'discipline' that characterized Christian society in time past will return, including the beating of children? I do not possess a crystal ball. But I hope the Spirit of God, obliged to concentrate her work outside the churches because the churches have their shutters up, will be triumphant in the twenty-first century. She is, after all, the Spirit of freedom who blows where she wills. She is the Spirit of truth who will set us free. The Church must be willing to learn before it tries to teach. That will mean going to those places of uncertainty and risk where it does not wish to go. It must learn genuine humility, willing to be taught by outsiders and people who are different. It must learn to relax and not have such an exalted and oppressive view of its own role and responsibility. It must learn the language of love from those who by trial and error have some competence in it. It must learn to cooperate with good wherever it is to be found instead of believing its own system to be synonymous with good. Every society and every system will have its victims. Sex and knowledge about sex is not the answer to healthy living. It is only part of the answer. Imperfection will not cease. Misunderstanding will not cease. Sin will not cease. There will still be that absence of kindness that my father cherished before everything. There will be sexual victims as well as other victims, requiring long-term friendship and care. It may be that along these lines the churches will discover new roles. We need fewer churches, and those churches more focussed on loving and informed care for the wounded. Places where people will not be judged and where the notice board that says "All are welcome" will at last tell the truth.

The sharp winds of change are now sweeping our land-
It's you, God, we recognize your Spirit's hand;
She's waking our dull, unadventurous faith,
And nothing is certain or rigid or safe.

(Chorus) Welcome God, welcome new, welcome Spirit again;
In your life, in your love, never one day the same;
We join, as your family, to work and adore,
Your great world to care for, enjoy and explore.

2) We thank you for leading us right where we are,
For giving the courage to do and to dare,
For lifting our hearts when our feelings were low,
Your laughter to echo, your beauty to show.

3) Through many a torment and many an ill,
You've led us through valleys and over each hill,
We've marked pleasant vistas and frightening scenes,
But the country we long for will outshine our dreams.

4) Today you are with us, inspiring our song,
You bind us together to know we belong;
We welcome the sharp winds, disturbing our ways,
Sure sign of your Spirit, God- yours be the praise!

(Inspired by John Gwilym Jones 'Fe chwythodd yr awel..'
and the tune 'To God be the glory' W.H.Doane

OTHER BOOKS BY
JOHN HENSON

GOOD AS NEW – A RADICAL RETELLING OF THE CHRISTIAN SCRIPTURES.
'O Books' Hard cover; paper back & e-books. ISBN: 978 1 90504 711 6
> *'A presentation of extraordinary power'* Rowan Williams, former Archbisop of Canterbury.

OTHER TEMPTATIONS OF JESUS
'John Hunt Publishing' ISBN 1 84298 140 4
> *'I recommend this work to anyone who enjoys an unpredictable reading of scripture'* John Rackley, President of the Baptist Union of Great Britain 2003

OTHER COMMUNIONS OF JESUS
'O Books' ISBN 1 905047 49 5
> *In this new edition of John Henson's classic, we are again confronted with the question, Have we been doing it right?*

OTHER PRAYERS OF JESUS
'O Books' ISBN 978 1 84694 079 8
> *'To read John Henson is always to look at things from a fresh angle. Sometimes with a jolt, he opens up new and earthly glimpses of God's grace'.*
> Peter West, Christian Aid area co-ordinator.

BAD ACTS OF THE APOSTLES
'O Books' ISBN 978 1 84694 169 6
> *'..once John Henson's revolutionary insights and deliciously subversive words enter our minds, they demand as response.'* Peterson Toscano U.S.A. Christian theatrical performance activist and Quaker.

THE GAY DISCIPLE – Jesus' friend tells it his own way
'O Books' ISBN 13: 978 1 84694 001 9 ISBN 10: 1 84694 001 X
> *'Original, provocative and gripping. Henson brings the biblical documents alive in startling and compelling ways'.* Dr Nicola Slee, Queen's College, Birmingham. UK.

WIDE AWAKE WORSHIP –
Hymns and Prayers Renewed for the 21st Century.
'O Books' ISBN 978 1 84694 392 8

> *'I always hoped that someone with sensitivity would rework some of the fine older hymns which need a bit of burnishing, and am delighted to find that John Henson has done this so well. I look forward to using them.'* John Bell, The Iona Community.

MAKE CHRISTMAS REAL
Authorhouse. ISBN 978 1 4969 7894

> *'Read this book and experience a more loving celebration of 'God with us' than you ever thought possible'* Gregory Spayd, Pastor serving St.Genevieve Parish, Corpus Christi, Texas. May be obtained from the author.

OTHER FRIENDS OF JESUS
Matador. ISBN 978 1789014 457

> *This is John Henson at his best. Steeped in the very best research, OTHER FRIENDS OF JESUS somehow manages to be provocative, profound, challenging, and yet imminently accessible to all. And it is a true revelation that leaves you thinking, "Well, of course!" and at the same time marveling, "I've never thought of it that way before!" Like only a few can do, John leads readers to a new dimension of Jesus, as deeply, intentionally, and strategically connected and interconnected. It will have readers looking at the tapestry and scale of Jesus' human interactions afresh.* Revd David Henson M.A., Trinity Episcopalian Church, Ashville, North Carolina USA.